Lincoln

The Making of a Leader

www.LincolnTheMakingOfALeader.com

Glen Aubrey

Author, Publisher, Professional Musician,
Emmy ® Award Winner, Consultant

Creative Team Publishing
Fort Worth, Texas

© 2017 by Glen Aubrey.

All rights reserved. No part of this book may be reproduced, stored in a retrieval system or transmitted in any form or by any means without the prior written permission of the publisher, except by a reviewer who may quote brief passages in a review distributed through electronic media, or printed in a newspaper, magazine, or journal.

Disclaimers:
- Due diligence has been exercised to obtain written permission for use of references or quotes where required. Additional quotes or references are subject to the Fair Use Doctrine. Where additional references or quotes may require source credit, upon written certification that such a claim is accurate, credit for use will be noted on the book's website.
- The opinions and conclusions expressed are solely those of the author and/or the individuals and entities represented and are limited to the facts, experiences, and circumstances involved. No professional, psychological, or medical advice is implied, stated, or offered in any way. You are encouraged to seek professional help, education, advice, and counsel should you desire to learn more about human behavior, personality, or medically related topics. Certain names and related circumstances have been changed to protect confidentiality. All stories where names are mentioned are used with the permission of the parties involved, if applicable. Any resemblance to past or current people, places, circumstances, or events not a part of the Lincoln history is purely coincidental.

ISBN: 978-0-9979519-1-2

PUBLISHED BY CREATIVE TEAM PUBLISHING
www.CreativeTeamPublishing.com
Ft. Worth, Texas
Printed in the United States of America

Glen Aubrey

www.glenaubrey.com

Author and Publisher

Leadership Is – How to Build Your Legacy
Industrial Strength Solutions Build Successful Work Teams!
Core Teams Work Their Principles and Practices
L.E.A.D. – Learning, Education, Action, Destiny
Leadership Works – Advanced Study Guide for L.E.A.D.
Lincoln, Leadership and Gettysburg – Defining Moments of Greatness
Go From the Night – Journeys of Thought, Meditations on Life
Freedom Light – Expressions of Hope and Evidence
Lessons of War – Lincoln's Second Inaugural Address, Leadership at Gettysburg
Lincoln's Leadership – If You Want Success, Lead Like This
Lincoln's Advice for America in the 21st Century – His Words Still Speak
Lincoln – The Making of a Leader

2012 Emmy® Award Winning Songwriter and Arranger
National Academy of Television Arts & Sciences
Pacific Southwest Chapter
Thirty-eighth Annual Pacific Southwest Emmy® Awards

Glen Aubrey, Piano Keyboard Art © 2017 Glen Aubrey
All Rights Reserved
Special thanks to artist Debi, '77 aka Debi Musick
http://newbeginningshome.org/
Debi, I am grateful to you!

Lincoln

The Making of a Leader

Glen Aubrey

Endorsements on behalf of Glen Aubrey

Books and Professional Consultation Services

Cal Thomas, Syndicated Columnist, Fox News Contributor
Core Teams Work

"There are two roads to business and personal success. One pursues success as an end in itself, often poisoning relationships and corrupting morals; the other road is paved with sound and proven principles which succeed without poisoning relationships and without the guilt. Glen Aubrey shows us how to succeed in business and in life by taking the second and better road."

Seth Godin, Author, *Purple Cow*
Industrial Strength Solutions

"No fancy theories here, just the realities of working with (and leading) teams. This book will make you think—hard—about what it means to lead."

Endorsements

Harold Holzer
Senior Vice President for Public Affairs
The Metropolitan Museum of Art
Lincoln's Advice for America in the 21st Century — His Words Still Speak

"Is Lincoln relevant today — and if so, how? Glen Aubrey offers a no-nonsense, highly useful guide to learning from America's greatest president. You may not agree with every conclusion he makes — I don't — but his ear for the useful and inspiring is amazing. Glen is a fine teacher, and leaders and prospective leaders should have this book as required reading."

Steven B. Wiley, CEO & Founder, The Lincoln Leadership Institute at Gettysburg
www.GettysburgLeadership.com
Lincoln's Advice for America in the 21st Century — His Words Still Speak

"Everyone needs a mentor — why not have that mentor be Abraham Lincoln? Now, thanks to Glen Aubrey's *Lincoln's Advice for America in the 21st Century – His Words Still Speak*, you can! Aubrey provides for the modern reader a virtual blueprint to applying Lincoln's principles and proclamations to today's world. We don't learn from our experiences; rather, we learn from reflecting upon our experiences. Aubrey gives us much to reflect about."

Endorsements

Malcolm Dougherty, Director, California Department of Transportation (Caltrans)
Core Teams Work

"As a leader in a large organization I realize my executive managers are experts and leaders in their own right, but it is my job to ensure they function as an efficient, high performing team. *Core Teams Work* explores the dynamics of teamwork that can either help or hinder the entire organization's performance…"

Major General Robert F. Dees, United States Army, Retired
Lessons of War — Lincoln's Second Inaugural Address, Leadership at Gettysburg

"*Lessons of War — Lincoln's Second Inaugural Address, Leadership at Gettysburg* is a tremendous contribution to the art and science of strategic leadership, as viewed through the crucible of human conflict. Glen Aubrey's insightful reflections into President Lincoln's Second Inaugural Address, particularly how Abraham Lincoln 'set the conditions' for our nation's fateful transition from civil war to lasting peace, is critically relevant to the daunting challenges faced by our current senior political and military leaders, as they also determine how best to turn swords into plowshares in Iraq, Afghanistan, and beyond."

Endorsements

**Kevin D. Bouren, Major, U.S. Army, Executive Officer,
Directorate of Admissions
United States Military Academy at West Point**
*Lessons of War—Lincoln's Second Inaugural Address,
Leadership at Gettysburg*

"With his clear and engaging style, Glen once again delivers a fascinating and indispensable examination of leadership, this time through the lens of an American hero. Lincoln's powerful legacy of strong leadership in war, founded upon his reverence for God, is a sterling model for every leader. Military and civilian leaders must apply the timeless lessons gleaned from Glen's analysis, particularly during this age of enduring conflict.

"The Directorate of Admissions at West Point is proud to endorse Glen Aubrey and the CTRG organization, and the great work they have done for us... One element that has truly had a profound impact on our team was the formulation of our Values, Vision, Mission, and Message. After ratifying this document as a team, it is now used to measure our performance across a broad range of activities. Our Core Values have also helped us to screen potential employees to determine if they are the right fit for us as they determine if we are the right fit for them. Invaluable.

"Glen Aubrey is a tremendous facilitator, mentor, leader, and team-builder. We are greatly indebted to him and CTRG for their timely recommendations and priceless input to our team. Without a doubt, we will go farther and do better now that we have partnered with Glen's incredible team of professionals. We give our deepest gratitude and appreciation to you (Glen) for investing in us."

Dr. Rick Hicks, President, Operation Mobilization, USA
Leadership Is — How to Build Your Legacy
"We have a choice in how we lead. Glen Aubrey, in his book *Leadership Is—*, lays out a road map to navigate these choices. As we follow his advice and become more intentional in our dealings with others, we are shown how to 'Lead well, and build people for life.'

"It is a privilege for me to serve as a reference for Creative Team Resources Group… Glen has incredibly strong commitment to building teams… Many in the marketplace are aware of the need for effectiveness of team-building principles. The issues of building trust, educating, giving people parameters, having accountability, and freeing them up in their areas of creativity provide a work environment that can be healthier, happier and more effective in the long run.

"One of the effective tools that I have seen Glen use is this team-building process which builds strong, healthy, work relationships. That is, it helps people understand how they relate one to another, what their roles are, and how they need each other to fulfill the overall task as a team. It is easy to talk about team-building and relationship-building in the workforce. But to actually accomplish these tasks through the consulting process is quite difficult. I have seen Glen come into a situation with a very results-oriented perspective and an analytical approach, and be able to take the theory and apply it practically and effectively.

"If your situation warrants giving attention to the issue of team-building, I would recommend Creative Team Resources Group to you without reservation…"

Jerald Coleman, IT Director, Health and Human Services Agency, County of San Diego
Core Teams Work

"Like many organizations with technology-oriented staff, we like to attack and solve problems. *Leadership Is—* showed us how to open lines of communication. *Industrial Strength Solutions* reminded us to 'close the loop' to ensure our tasks were complete. *Core Teams Work* provides us with the principles and practices to promote effective communication amongst ourselves and with our customers."

Rick Perrotta, CEO, Rubicon Technology Group
Industrial Strength Solutions

"Principles of leadership, team building, character and change are the vital determining factors in today's competitive business landscape, and the critical characteristics in today's flatter world. This is value-added differentiation for business products, solutions, and relationships. Mature and potential leaders will absorb and commit to practicing the principles and methodologies outlined here which are reinforced with excellent 'real world' examples."

David A. Fisher, Partner, K&L Gates LLP
Leadership Is — How to Build Your Legacy
"With great difficulty, many have analyzed and some have well defined at least the qualities of leadership. Glen Aubrey superbly takes his readers into the more challenging domain of how to accomplish it.

"When we first met and I first considered retaining CTRG nothing could have prepared me for what I would learn or the results that would be achieved to date. We would do it again not only with no hesitation, but happily..."

John D. Kirby, Colonel (Retired), Vietnam Combat Veteran 1st Cavalry Division (Airmobile); Subsequently Attorney-at-Law, Litigation
Lessons of War — Lincoln's Second Inaugural Address, Leadership at Gettysburg
"Leadership — real, enduring leadership — is shown in *Lessons of War — Lincoln's Second Inaugural Address, Leadership at Gettysburg* to be that which is firmly grounded in and based upon reality and truth, coupled with genuine caring for those being led. This, in turn, leads to the best

preparation for and conduct of the conflict. Glen Aubrey carries forward these critical leadership principals, and shows how to succeed in the next and final phase of every conflict—the ending of the conflict, with an accompanying establishment of genuine peace, or as close to genuine peace as is humanly possible, and Godly allowed. A must read for anyone who wishes his or her own conflicts, personal or organizational, to end well."

**Alisa Edwards, Realtor, Dwell Well Realty,
San Diego, California and Los Angeles, California**

"I am a Realtor. I work for myself, considered an independent contractor in the State of California. It was interesting to me once we got into the team training, that I am part of several teams in my work environment. I do have a core team of people that I work with towards a common goal in each transaction. The tricks and tools I learned have helped to solidify the foundation of each team I work with and the way we communicate, as well as why we do what we do. I would recommend your class series to anyone looking to polish team communication and goal clarification. Thank you so much for all the coaching, it has provided a wonderful foundation for my everyday life, both work and home. You and your team are doing great things!"

Endorsements

Thomas R. Clark, RPh, MHS, Director of Policy and Advocacy
American Society of Consultant Pharmacists

"Your consulting services, along with Core Team training and Leadership Investment training, have been extremely useful to us... Your expertise, and especially your passion and commitment, have set an example for our staff and shown us how to put into practice the principles that you have been teaching. The training materials you supplied have provided a continuing reminder of those principles and have been an important part of the package of services for our company. The net impact of your services has been to improve working relationships and to provide key leaders with the knowledge and skills to maintain this improvement in the future... I would certainly encourage any business to take advantage of the services provided by your company."

Barry E. Willey, Colonel (Retired), U.S. Army
Author, *Out of the Valley* **(Officers' Christian Fellowship, 2007)**
Lessons of War — Lincoln's Second Inaugural Address, Leadership at Gettysburg

"Many Americans have never encountered Lincoln's Second Inaugural Address, nor fully appreciate the strategic importance of the Battle of Gettysburg in our nation's history. Glen Aubrey's *Lessons of War — Lincoln's Second Inaugural Address, Leadership at Gettysburg* brings both of these historically significant events together in a poignant way. He helps us see clearly that seeking peaceful resolution is the ultimate aim of those forced to participate in war and that good leaders 'choose the best ways to conduct and conclude it.' Aubrey's insights are captivating and compelling. Examples of sound leadership lessons and principles abound in every chapter. Former, current and aspiring leaders would be wise to learn them, savor them ... and apply them as they lead. This is a future classic."

Stephen M. Annis, Sergeant (Retired),
United States Air Force
Vietnam War Veteran 1966 – 1970
Executive Vice President and Chief Financial Officer,
Valley Republic Bank
Lessons of War — Lincoln's Second Inaugural Address,
Leadership at Gettysburg

"As an avid student of the nation-changing event we know as the Battle of Gettysburg, Glen Aubrey has now completed his second study of the lessons to be learned from that conflict and, more importantly, the lessons to be learned from studying the genius that was and is Abraham Lincoln. In *Lessons of War — Lincoln's Second Inaugural Address, Leadership at Gettysburg*, Glen opens our eyes to the message of hope, commitment, and faith in God that Lincoln so skillfully wove into his Second Inaugural Address. You cannot read this book without gaining enormous insight into Abraham Lincoln — the man. Glen then takes that insight and develops a clear understanding of how those truths can be used to enrich our own lives and leadership styles today."

Deanna Christiansen, Author
Notes on a Flight Home
and
Plantings in Poetry, Essay, and Song
www.DeannaChristiansen.com
Lincoln's Advice for America in the 21st Century —
His Words Still Speak

"If we can listen to Lincoln today, and apply what we reflect on to our contemporary times, we tap an irreplaceable resource of wisdom we otherwise to our risk lack, to become those thoughtful, informed, sacrificially patriotic citizens our Democracy requires. Glen Aubrey fills our urgent requirement by this book."

About this Book

Lincoln – The Making of a Leader briefly examines a history of the life and surroundings of Abraham Lincoln, incorporating viewpoints from two men who knew Mr. Lincoln intimately: William H. Herndon and Ward H. Lamon. Reading what these two gentlemen wrote regarding Lincoln from their personal and professional perspectives in the years immediately following Lincoln's assassination, helps us glean closer and hopefully more accurate understandings of Lincoln's unique contributions to American history—who he was as a person as well as the immense impact he had—and the experiences and life lessons that served to shape him. Even a brief examination of Lincoln must include a look at the character, experiences, education, environment, marriage and family life, business dealings, personality traits, and leadership of the man who became the country's sixteenth president.

Lincoln, the man, was complex. The reader is encouraged to delve into much more thorough research than what is able to be presented here, to discover what scholars have declared made Lincoln who he was and became. It's likely a never-ending quest for knowledge of not only what Lincoln did, but why he did it. What made Mr. Lincoln the leader he was shown to become throughout the varied stages of his life—both before and during his White House years?

The book asks, "What makes any person a leader?" "What can we learn from Lincoln's life and experience that may contribute to the people of our day who aspire to or assume leadership roles, to become leaders in their environments and organizations for the right reasons, best causes, producing meritorious results?"

Lincoln served our nation during the Civil War. One cannot really venture too far down the path of study and any examination of Lincoln without seeking to learn about that horrific, yet some would say necessary national conflict: its causes, catastrophic sacrifices, the lingering effects of brutal conflict, as well as some of the incidents within the war that shaped and continue to shape the nation—the Gettysburg campaign and the Gettysburg Address are two examples—but there are so many more, certainly including the 13th Amendment that abolished slavery, an Amendment to the Constitution which Lincoln desperately desired but did not live to see.

The making of a leader combines life experiences, formal learning, true-to-life applications, multiple environments, trial, error, successes, and failures. Ultimately leaders make choices about how to lead and how their desired achievements are to be won. Distractions can be many, but should not dissuade from a higher call if the call is worthy. Motives and methods remain vital considerations. The core of the person and his or her personality traits are factors, too.

What drives any leader and why? How does a leader evaluate success or failure?

Perhaps you will discover solid truths that can help you become the kind of leader you truly want to be. Perhaps you will learn several factors that made Lincoln the man and leader he was shown to be, and how much impact his leadership had upon our country's history, and continues to have on our ongoing existence.

Credits in Order of Appearance

Eagle Drawing by Justin Aubrey © 2017
is used with permission.

*****

Excerpts from *Lincoln's Leadership * If You Want Success, Lead Like This* © 2012 are used by permission.

*****

References and quotes from
Herndon's Lincoln, The True Story of a Great Life
The History and Personal Recollections of Abraham Lincoln
By William H. Herndon For Twenty Years His Friend and
Law Partner and Jesse William Weik, A. M.
Volumes I, II, III, Herndon's Lincoln Publishing Company,
Publishers, Springfield, Illinois, 1888.
Public Domain.

*****

Lincoln's First Autobiography, June, 1858.
Access Oct. 12, 2017
https://www.nps.gov/abli/learn/news/abraham-lincoln-autobiography.htm
Public Domain.

*****

Credits in Order of Appearance

Lincoln's Second Autobiography, 1859.
Accessed October 12, 2017
https://www.nps.gov/abli/learn/news/abraham-lincoln-autobiography.htm
Public Domain.

*****

Quotes from March 3, 1837 "Illinois House Journal", Pages 817 and 818, a protest entered upon the "Illinois House Journal" Abraham Lincoln with Dan Stone.
Public Domain.

*****

Quotes from 1847 Documents: the 'Journal' and 'Congressional Globe.'
Public Domain.

*****

Article I, Section 8 of the Constitution of the United States.
Public Domain.

*****

Quoting from a photograph of Lincoln's early handwriting is accessed from *Lincoln A Picture Story of His Life*
By Stefan Lorant, Revised and Enlarged Edition, Harper & Brothers, New York, © 1957, Page 130.

*****

Credits in Order of Appearance

Photographs of Lincoln Square, Springfield, Illinois, and Lincoln Home, Springfield, Illinois, are taken by the author.

*****

Photograph of Portrait of Mary Lincoln is from a newspaper clipping owned by the author, dated October 18, 1896.
Public Domain.

*****

Quotes from *The Marine Bank – The Story of the Oldest Bank in Illinois* by author Paul M. Angle (b. 1900, d. 1975).
Public Domain.

*****

Quote regarding how Mary Lincoln handled money: http://talkingcents.consumercredit.com/2014/02/17/mary-todd-lincoln-compulsive-shopper-severe-debt-problems/ Accessed May 27, 2017.

*****

Photo dated August 8, 1860: A Great Republican Rally in front of Lincoln's home in Springfield, Illinois following his nomination in 1860.
Public Domain.

*****

Credits in Order of Appearance

Quoting Lincoln on his signing a photograph to
Mrs. Lucy G. Speed, thanking her for the gift of a Bible,
noted in *Lincoln A Picture Story of His Life* By Stefan Lorant,
Revised and Enlarged Edition,
Harper & Brothers, New York, © 1957, Page 19.

*****

The Washington Post on Americans losing 40% of wealth:
https://www.washingtonpost.com/business/economy/fed-americans-wealth-dropped-40-percent/2012/06/11/gJQAlIsCVV_story.html

*****

The poem, *Mortality*, written in 1824 by William Knox.
Public Domain.

*****

Quotation of Esther 4:14b is from the Holy Bible
(Authorized King James Version of 1611).
Public Domain

*****

Reference to Ward Hill Lamon:
https://en.wikipedia.org/wiki/Ward_Hill_Lamon.
Accessed September 27, 2017.

*****

Credits in Order of Appearance

Quotations from *The Life of Abraham Lincoln; from His Birth to his Inauguration as President.*
By Ward H. Lamon.
With Illustrations
Boston: James R. Osgood And Company,
(Late Ticknor and Fields, and Field, Osgood, & Co.), 1872.
Public Domain.

*****

Excerpts and adaptations from
Surviving Obama's Economy – Challenge vs. Opportunity
By Harry Stadille with Glen Aubrey © 2012 are used by permission of the Harry Stadille family and Creative Team Publishing.

*****

Introduction:
It Takes a Secure Person with a Strong Personality to Tell Truthful and Compelling Stories for the Good of the Listener—Even if a Story Pokes Fun at the Storyteller

Secure leaders often tell stories to their followers to illustrate salient points they want to make. Often they relate anecdotes that mean the most to them, sometimes using their own foibles as illustrations of what to do and what not to do. The hope is that the "moral" or central meaning of any story will resonate with followers as much as the story itself does.

A leader who relates a story enjoys it when a follower "gets it" and has his or her own "ah ha" moment—whether producing a solemn reaction or a humorous outburst. A collection of those remembrances and stories are the seeds of great and sometimes life changing lessons where truth is embedded in reality, and people learn from shared history.

Lincoln was a master storyteller. His storytelling was unique. One thing that made his stories memorable was that they were anchored to real lives of common people and the causes of their day. Read and study hundreds of books on Lincoln's life and pilgrimage and you can't avoid this fact.

Working within towns up and down the judicial circuit in Illinois, from his beginning days as a lawyer, it was not uncommon for the judge, lawyers (from both sides), and other interested parties at the close of a day of judicial proceedings, to adjourn to a nearby watering hole and swap stories until late at night. Lincoln's manner in these early days was familiar among frontiersmen; he was coarse, blunt, but respectful while cloaking his stories in humorous anecdotes of the day. People loved hearing him.

When he was elected to the highest office of the land, President Lincoln didn't stop telling his stories—in fact he often used them to illustrate momentous truths, lighten up a situation, or change the direction of a conversation. These stories were born of memories and experiences of common men and women, and familiar themes were intertwined all the way through them.

These tales served the president and his listeners well. In a highly charged and deeply depressing time of war he would often stop in the middle of a cabinet discourse to tell his cabinet members a story or a joke. The fact that he would do this was well known. In fact, there were times when he was severely criticized and mocked for telling humorous stories when so many men on both sides of the conflict were dying. Storytelling helped Lincoln remain sane and grounded and often provided just the release a moment of angst or momentous judgment may have needed.

One story Lincoln is said to have told often was about his homeliness. Most people thought Lincoln was not very good looking. He was tall, angular, rugged, and uncouth in some of his mannerisms. His frame was gangly, his hair often uncombed, his clothes didn't fit very well especially in his youth and early career, and he hailed from the "backwoods." All in all, the image most people had of Lincoln was not one of a handsome and cultured man.

One variation of a story he told on himself goes like this: Lincoln was walking alone on a country road one day when a man approached him, stopped him, gazed into his eyes and up and down his face. Presently the man presented Lincoln with a knife, stating, "I want to give this knife to you; this is your personal property." Lincoln responded, "No, I have never owned a knife like this; you must be mistaken." The stranger replied, "No, there is no mistake. The person who gave me this knife said I should give it to anyone I found who was uglier than me, and you sir, certainly fit that description!"

Lincoln's focus in his storytelling was often a truth that the common man would understand. His purpose was to relate to his audience, regardless of size or makeup, some of the history that all of them shared, and his responsibility was to open up opportunities for gems of truth to be uncovered and appreciated—humorous or not.

A responsibility to learn from history means, of course, that we must know our history well enough in order to learn from it. That responsibility often embraces uncovering a shared memory and retelling it.

If you're the leader or a committed follower: become well acquainted with the history your group or team should embrace and from which they could learn. Then give them a story now and then to illustrate a truth, embrace a lesson, improve an environment, or change a circumstance. You'll likely be surprised the positive effects assuming that responsibility can produce.

The phrase, "Let me tell you a story…" carries great weight when it attracts the attention of those who would benefit from the telling of a tale, hearing it told, learning its value, and laughing a little or a lot, too, if that's the intent and what is needed.

How good a storyteller are you? Are you personally strong enough to tell truthful and compelling stories to help make an environment better, even if you get your audience to laugh at you?

How convinced are you that meaningful storytelling for the good of those with whom you associate should be a part of your person, personality, and leadership?

Table of Contents

Endorsements on behalf of Glen Aubrey   *7*

About this Book   *19*

Credits in Order of Appearance   *23*

Introduction:
    It Takes a Secure Person with a Strong
    Personality to Tell Truthful and Compelling
    Stories for the Good of the Listener—
    Even if a Story Pokes Fun at the Storyteller   *29*

*****

1
    Personality Doesn't Drive—It Is Driven   *37*

2
    An Upbringing and Early Career Few May
    Experience or Endure   *45*

3
    Character on Display in Springfield   *61*

4
    Who Was Mary Todd and What Was Her
    Influence on Lincoln?   *73*

5
    Early Marriage, Financial Hardships, Home Life   *81*

Table of Contents

6
    Ambition *101*

7
    Overcoming—Understanding Call and Capability *121*

8
    Closing Thoughts *135*

*****

About the Author *137*

Products and Services *141*

Acknowledgments *143*

Eagle Drawing by Justin Aubrey.
© 2017 by Justin Aubrey. All Rights Reserved.

I have always enjoyed this pencil drawing by my son. Leaders soar above distractions while expressing nobility and dedication to their cause. Perhaps you are a leader in the making who desires to soar in strength and provide great leadership to those who follow you.

1

Personality Doesn't Drive— It Is Driven

During the 1980s, 1990s, and well into the 21st century, a company I lead, Creative Team Resources Group (CTRG, www.ctrg.com), actively engaged and continues to practice team and leadership development and effective communication improvement, providing consultation services to a wide variety of organizations: for-profit, nonprofit, public and private sector firms, including government ... all the way from local (city, county) to state and national (federal) levels.

Several books have been published through Creative Team Publishing, (CTP) (please see this website: www.CreativeTeamPublishing.com), in affiliation with CTRG, offering curriculum, instruction, and ongoing investment and inspiration to teams with whom CTRG is privileged to work. Dealing with literally thousands of employees, managers, executive team members, and leaders and followers of all kinds, we confront and engage people who desire improvement, who face challenges no matter their product or cause. We help them win.

People are people … the possibilities and challenges are similar regardless of the organization or its mission. Benefits are similar, too, when a team chooses to positively engage and change their behaviors for the better. The key word here is "chooses." We have many choices; one is how much we allow personality to affect us regardless of circumstances or events. The degrees of demonstration and effects of personality are choices.

The results of behavioral changes that are made from desires to improve versus forced improvements (usually policy-dictated) are remarkable. Put another way: people are stronger when they change because they want to, not when they have to. Desire is always preferable to dictate and choices precede results.

Actually, the same truth goes for individuals, whether or not they are involved in a group or serve on a team. Principles are truths that do not change. The message remains the same, though the methods of presenting and living within truth-filled environments often vary with times, cultures, circumstances, and the reality of that which never seems to change: change, itself.

Teams or groups of individuals who are tasked to work together and who want to improve team thought and action, and produce exemplary results, are greatly helped when they embrace a primary goal as they build their team's structure, function, and intent. Teams who want to work together benefit greatly when they create and implement what we call, core teams.

The meaning of this term *Core Team* is highly significant. In brief:

The Core Team

C   Consistency — proven reliability

O   Obedience to shared core values upon which we agree

R   Right Relationships, where a relationship is defined as the decision one makes about another's success

E   Example, realizing that providing one is not optional; the question is, "What kind of example do you provide?"

T   Trust — no requirement is higher in importance. There are many kinds of trust. The first is that trust is granted at the beginning of any relationship; it is then earned and proven or disproven over time; when trust is violated, the trust covenant is often severed; and there is only one way to start building trust again: it must once more be

	granted freely before a trust relationship can be proven or disproven over time.
E	The Essentials of Composite Nature: what constitutes a person at their core. These are composed of experience, education, and environment.
A	Accountability: relational and functional
M	Methods which compose the actions of the Core Team

Throughout the processes of creating and activating core teams, personality is a topic often addressed because it must be. The study of personality types and traits, and the applications of these designations or labels often are used, ostensibly, to help people know themselves as well as know better the others around them so everyone can "relate" to each other and in doing so, hopefully achieve more. Studies are voluminous as to how learning and understanding personality types and traits impact or reveal who people are and the reasons for their behaviors.

Many of the organizations with which CTRG has experience continue to use extensive and expensive tests to determine their employees', managers', and leaders' personality types and traits. These tests, by definition, are supposed to determine whether person A and person B can get along, work together well, or whether because of personality differences these two should not be closely tied together or even see or associate with each other at all. CTRG does not administer these tests, though we often have had to deal with the expected and unexpected results from time to time when these tests are utilized in business, producing health or dysfunction — many times the latter.

Well, let's face some hard truth:

While labels of personality traits can be beneficial when used correctly, alternatively, they can be used as excuses to justify failure if for some reason two or more people do not want to work together well or do not desire to dwell or relate closely with each other. You know the conclusion: "These two people can't play in the same sandbox."

In several of our consulting engagements for over thirty years, we were asked to observe and assist organizations to confront negative trends where a client's team members would hide behind personality differences in order to avoid facing and resolving blatant dysfunction. Their purpose appeared to be to avoid dealing with problems. They did this for many reasons. Among them: plain laziness, insecurity, fears of revealing their own negative character traits, blatant disregard for other team members' or a company's welfare or production, or rampant "I don't care" attitudes, too often accompanied by subversively destructive activities. The bottom line: these people wanted to ignore personal ownership of responsibility. In these sub-work environments, instead of changing behaviors and maturing, people so inclined would employ tactics of blaming each other, finding fault in personality or cultural differences, and label these as "reasons" for dysfunction. They would choose to be content with living and working in environments of selfishness, discourtesy, and isolation which they often created, encouraged and to which they contributed. Work environments, products, processes, and profits would all suffer. These conditions, unfortunately, were all too common. They still are.

Yes, while benefits can exist in the study of personalities to gain greater knowledge with lofty and right goals of improvements, detriments can also be prevalent. Used inappropriately, personality descriptions can become hedges or hiding places designed to shield chronic irresponsibility and foster an absence of dedication on the part of individuals who do not desire to act responsibly. These people shun contributions to the progress of their core team or company. In these circumstances, we witness a violation of the "O" of the Core Team values: obedience to shared core values upon which the team has agreed.

You may be pleased or relieved to learn at this juncture that this is not a book essentially about personality types, traits, and labels; far too much has already been written on that subject. It is not the intent of the author to regurgitate that information or offer statistical proofs here.

This is a book about seeing one person in particular accomplish much because he chose to *not* permanently allow descriptions of his personality or even other people's opinions of him to be harbingers of difficulty or failure for him. He refused to use his personality traits or other's opinions to define his limits, or to garner excuses for inactivity, even when times were hard. He succeeded, no matter what, during times of great pain, trial, and loss. He persevered. That person to whom I refer, of course, was Abraham Lincoln.

Sources of information of what people close to him observed are many. We will refer to some here. Stories and expressions from Mr. Lincoln himself are well known and can serve to illustrate one supremely important lesson: Personality does not drive, it is driven. No more excuses, though it must be recognized that personality tendencies and other people's opinions and actions do have impact. However, it is a *choice* as to how much or even whether one's personality or what others say about him or her should be allowed to dictate action and corresponding results.

Personality—a collection of characteristics that often are used to describe an individual—will be recognized and must be shaped, though some traits may appear to be inherited. Regardless of source, personality is driven by its owner.

For success to become reality, depending on how success is defined—and here it is defined as being so secure, unselfish, and sacrificial that one invests in others to help them achieve their dreams and goals*—personality traits must become subject to their owner. If that owner in his or her persona is to become as great a contributor or leader as possible, it is incumbent upon that person to use his or her personality traits as part of an arsenal of accomplishment, not as a collection of excuses for doing less or accomplishing nothing of value.

I realize that some of my readers, right now, will choose to disagree. No argument is desired or needed.

But, if you want more insight into Abraham Lincoln the person and the leader, you may want to continue your reading. He was impacted by his personality and the people around him for sure, but he rose to leadership greatness because he wanted it and worked for it, no matter what his "personality" characteristics may have illustrated, what others said about him, or the trials that punctuated his life and experience.

*Please see *Leadership Is—How to Build Your Legacy.* www.LeadershipIs.com

2

An Upbringing and Early Career Few May Experience or Endure

Lincoln has often been quoted as saying, "No man should grow so tall that his feet should leave the ground." Whether he said it or not, and he probably didn't, one interpretation of that pithy sentence could be that all of us walk the same earth no matter degrees of ambition, success, or failure. And we eventually have to "come down" no matter how high our stature becomes or we think it should be.

Lincoln is also quoted as saying, "God must have loved the common man; He made so many of them." No, we don't know if he actually said that one, either. What we do know is that Lincoln was an emerging leader during his formative years and throughout his law practice in Springfield, Illinois.

He came from the communities of the "common man." He identified with his people's roots long before and during his elections, twice, to the office of President of the United States. Myth was becoming mixed into reality as a common backwoodsman became elevated to the most powerful position of the land. He was a competent and competitive politician. He was a part of the people and culture that gave context to his upbringing and helped to define his career. He was a leader of unquestioned growing fame. He had personality quirks, and we'll see that he endured a tough home life. Millions of his fellow countrymen didn't like him, disagreed with him, and objected to his election. Some hated him. In fact, before the fall of Fort Sumter in 1861, these seven states had already seceded from the Union: Alabama, Florida, Georgia, Louisiana, South Carolina, Mississippi, and Texas. Throughout the Civil War he faced strong opposition, and eventually one of his enemies became his assassin.

"But, in a larger sense…" These words composed one of the many memorable phrases in the Gettysburg Address which Lincoln delivered on November 19, 1863, helping to define the causes and effects of the war. Lincoln had the ability to make highly complex truths simpler to hear, and to paint a realistic portrait of conditions that his countrymen, whether for and against him, could comprehend. This address is a superb example of complex simplicity.

William Herndon became Lincoln's Springfield law partner in 1844. He wrote *Herndon's Lincoln, The True Story of a Great Life*. His preface to this book is dated November 1, 1888. "A thread of the narrative of Lincoln's life runs through the work, but an especial [sic] feature is an analysis of the man and a portrayal of his attributes and

characteristics... The object of this work is to deal with Mr. Lincoln individually and domestically; as lawyer, as citizen, as statesman... Mr. Lincoln was my warm, devoted friend. I always loved him, and I revere his name to this day."
Pgs. x and xi from the Preface

In over fifty years of studying and dwelling on the life, leadership, and legacy of Abraham Lincoln, as well as collecting, reading, and re-reading hundreds of books, I continue to immerse myself in the knowledge of his life. I respect his leadership example, intelligence, and the causes he embraced. These contributed to his effectiveness along with his styles of communication which reached the masses.

His development started early. It is well known that as a youth he often read *Aesop's Fables*, Bunyan's *Pilgrim's Progress*, George Bancroft's *History of the United States*, Weems' *Life of Washington*, and the Bible.

There is no question Lincoln hungered for knowledge and to become "great." His ambition was tempered by difficult circumstances, but he pursued. He was not impressed with his own "story," and his first biography was short and to the point, written in June, 1858:

"Born, February 12, 1809, in Hardin County, Kentucky.
Education defective.
Profession, a lawyer.
Have been a captain of volunteers in Black Hawk war.

Postmaster at a very small office.
Four times a member of the Illinois legislature, and was a member of the lower house of Congress."

*****

Perhaps the most well-known biography was composed in 1859. Lincoln's own assessment of this biography: "There is not much of it, for the reason, I suppose, that there is not much of me."

I remember hearing this biography quoted several times as I was growing up, and reading it often. See if this account fascinates you as much as it has me. Following at least in part the counsel of lawyer William Herndon, "leaving the reader to form his own opinions", I will give you one of my own and let you craft yours: Lincoln was presented with far more opportunities to relish in his difficulties, allow them to hold him back, and remain an unknown backwoodsman, instead of rising as he did to great leadership despite the struggles.

Here is the account:

"I was born Feb. 12, 1809, in Hardin County, Kentucky. My parents were both born in Virginia, of undistinguished families—second families, perhaps I should say. My mother, who died in my tenth year, was of a family of the name of Hanks, some of whom now reside in Adams, and others in

Macon Counties, Illinois. My paternal grandfather, Abraham Lincoln, emigrated from Rockingham County, Virginia, to Kentucky, about 1781 or 2, where, a year or two later, he was killed by indians [sic], not in battle, but by stealth, when he was laboring to open a farm in the forest. His ancestors, who were Quakers, went to Virginia from Berks County, Pennsylvania. An effort to identify them with the New-England family of the same name ended in nothing more definite, than a similarity of Christian names in both families, such as Enoch, Levi, Mordecai, Solomon, Abraham, and the like.

"My father, at the death of his father, was but six years of age; and he grew up, litterally [sic] without education. He removed from Kentucky to what is now Spencer County, Indiana, in my eighth year. We reached our new home about the time the State came into the Union. It was a wild region, with many bears and other wild animals, still in the woods. There I grew up. There were some schools, so called; but no qualification was ever required of a teacher beyond 'readin, writin, and cipherin' to the Rule of Three. If a straggler supposed to understand latin [sic] happened to sojourn in the neighborhood, he was looked upon as a wizzard [sic]. There was absolutely nothing to excite ambition for education. Of course when I came of age I did not know much. Still somehow, I could read, write, and cipher to the Rule of Three; but that was all. I have not been to school since. The little advance I now have upon this store of education, I have picked up from time to time under the pressure of necessity."

It may be worthwhile for the reader to understand the Rule of Three. It's all about math and the processes of proportion. An internet search will help in the explanation. The point is this: young Abraham learned how to think and reason with concepts, numbers, and maxims, studied on his own because he hungered for knowledge and this in spite of a difficult upbringing.

"I was raised to farm work, which I continued till I was twenty-two. At twenty-one I came to Illinois, and passed the first year in Macon County. Then I got to New-Salem (at that time in Sangamon, now in Menard County), where I remained a year as a sort of Clerk in a store. Then came the Black-Hawk war; and I was elected a Captain of Volunteers—a success which gave me more pleasure than any I have had since. I went [sic] the campaign, was elated, ran for the Legislature the same year (1832) and was beaten—the only time I ever have been beaten by the people. The next, and three succeeding biennial elections, I was elected to the Legislature. I was not a candidate afterwards. During this Legislative period I had studied law, and removed to Springfield to practice it. In 1846 I was once elected to the lower House of Congress. Was not a candidate for re-election. From 1849 to 1854, both inclusive, practiced law more assiduously than ever before. Always a whig [sic] in politics, and generally on the whig [sic] electoral tickets, making active canvasses—I was losing interest in politics, when the repeal of the Missouri Compromise aroused me again. What I have done since then is pretty well known.

"If any personal description of me is thought desirable, it may be said, I am, in height, six feet, four inches, nearly; lean in flesh, weighing on an average one hundred and eighty pounds; dark complexion, with coarse black hair, and grey eyes—no other marks or brands recollected."

*****

Lincoln was elected to the Illinois House of Representatives in 1834. You are invited to carefully consider Lincoln's statement on slavery in 1837 when he was but twenty-eight years old.

"March 3, 1837, by a protest entered upon the 'Illinois House Journal' of that date, at pages 817 and 818, Abraham Lincoln, with Dan Stone, another representative of Sangamon, briefly defined his position on the slavery question; and so far as it goes, it was then the same that it is now. The protest is as follows:

'Resolutions upon the subject of domestic slavery having passed both branches of the General Assembly at its present session, the undersigned hereby protest against the passage of the same.

'They believe that the institution of slavery is founded on both injustice and bad policy, but that the promulgation of Abolition doctrines tends rather to increase than abate its evils.

'They believe that the Congress of the United States has no power under the Constitution to interfere with the institution of slavery in the different States.

'They believe that the Congress of the United States has the power, under the Constitution, to abolish slavery in the District of Columbia, but that the power ought not to be exercised unless at the request of the people of the District.

'The difference between these opinions and those contained in the above resolutions is their reason for entering this protest.

    Dan Stone,
    A Lincoln,
    "Representatives from the County of Sangamon."'"

I have been keenly impressed with the stand Mr. Lincoln took against a popular president in 1847. The United States had been at war with Mexico during the time and the American army was still in Mexico. A peace treaty ratification was coming in June, but Lincoln rightfully was opposed to what he deemed illegal foreign occupation by U.S. armed forces. It is a matter of record, in the 'Journal' and 'Congressional Globe' that he voted *for* all the supply measures for U.S. troops, but the same publications also show him voting that the war "was unnecessarily and unconstitutionally begun by the President of the United States." Bold words, and true.

Mr. Lincoln had asserted that the President had sent armed forces into Mexico and therefore provoked and provided the first hostile act that started the war.

The Constitution states that war powers were vested in the Congress, not the president. If and since that was true, the president's acts had been unconstitutional.

> Article I, Section 8 of The Constitution of the United States: The Congress shall have Power To lay and collect Taxes, Duties, Imposts and Excises, to pay the Debts and provide for the common Defence and general Welfare of the United States; but all Duties, Imposts and Excises shall be uniform throughout the United States;
> To borrow Money on the credit of the United States;
> To regulate Commerce with foreign Nations, and among the several States, and with the Indian Tribes;
> To establish an uniform Rule of Naturalization, and uniform Laws on the

subject of Bankruptcies throughout the United States;

To coin Money, regulate the Value thereof, and of foreign Coin, and fix the Standard of Weights and Measures;

To provide for the Punishment of counterfeiting the Securities and current Coin of the United States;

To establish Post Offices and post Roads;

To promote the Progress of Science and useful Arts, by securing for limited Times to Authors and Inventors the exclusive Right to their respective Writings and Discoveries;

To constitute Tribunals inferior to the supreme Court;

To define and punish Piracies and Felonies committed on the high Seas, and Offences against the Law of Nations;

<u>To declare War</u>, grant Letters of Marque and Reprisal, and make Rules concerning Captures on Land and Water;

To raise and support Armies, but no Appropriation of Money to that Use shall be for a longer Term than two Years;

To provide and maintain a Navy;

To make Rules for the Government and Regulation of the land and naval Forces;

To provide for calling forth the Militia to execute the Laws of the Union, suppress Insurrections and repel Invasions;

To provide for organizing, arming, and disciplining, the Militia, and for governing such Part of them as may be employed in the Service of the United States, reserving to the States respectively, the Appointment of the Officers, and the Authority of training the Militia according to the discipline prescribed by Congress;

To exercise exclusive Legislation in all Cases whatsoever, over such District (not exceeding ten Miles square) as may, by Cession of particular States, and the Acceptance of Congress, become the Seat of the Government of the United States, and to exercise like Authority over all Places purchased by the Consent of the Legislature of the State in which the Same shall be, for the Erection of Forts, Magazines, Arsenals, dock-Yards, and other needful Buildings;-- And To make all Laws which shall be necessary and proper for carrying into Execution the foregoing Powers, and all other Powers vested by this Constitution in the Government of the United States, or in any Department or Officer thereof.

(underline added)

What did standing for right entail when the more popular position was the opposite of the one Lincoln espoused? Great leaders know where they stand, can clearly articulate their positions, and will not back down even though what they believe may not be what a group in power may want to hear.

Leadership takes a stand when the leader bases his or her declarations on principle, moral truth, and the rule of law, *no matter what*.

*****

Lincoln had accomplished much as a citizen and politician before he debated Steven A. Douglas. The debates ran from August 21, 1858 through October 15, 1858 as part of the Illinois state election campaign. Expanding national prominence was to accompany Lincoln largely as a result of these debates.

These provided a platform of introduction of Lincoln to the masses and the times were ripe that engulfed the controversy regarding slavery in America, whether its presence was right or wrong, to be protected, extended into new territories, or not.

The debates were lengthy, comprehensive, and at times entertaining—and they clearly showed the differences between the two candidates. Look at this schedule, all in

1858 and all in Illinois. Talk about pursuing the opportunities to present truth! This schedule was grueling by some standards and completely unlike the debate formats and timeframes we are used to in contemporary election processes. You are encouraged to see the texts of these interchanges. They can be accessed at this website: www.AbahamLincolnAssociation.org, and the Abraham Lincoln Association.*

*These writings of Lincoln have been published as *The Collected Works of Abraham Lincoln*. The copyright to *The Collected Works of Abraham Lincoln* is owned by the Abraham Lincoln Association.

The Lincoln-Douglas debate locations and dates:

1. Ottawa, August 21
2. Freeport, August 27
3. Jonesboro, September 15
4. Charleston, September 18
5. Galesburg, October 7
6. Quincy, October 13
7. Alton, October 15

In contemporary elections we have learned to expect soundbites from the media. Politicians play to this expectation knowing that soundbites compose the majority of what the media offers. The media provides them and these brief contributions are often driven by ratings and money.

To some, this soundbite practice is irritating if not disgusting. Those thirsting for more in-depth information are part of a populace who *wants* to hear more. To others, a soundbite mentality is permissible if not preferred because of what some have termed the "dumbing down" of the American citizen, concluding that the vast population will only remember the soundbite anyway, and it would cost too much airtime to showcase anything more than a two or three minute answer in a debate setting or a reference on a news program.

The tendency to provide merely capsule news in the form of soundbites may be shortchanging the American voter when soundbites are packaged as *the* news. I, for one, would like to hear more from the people we are charged or challenged to consider in an election. Covering rallies in their entirety may help, but balanced coverage of opposing candidates is required if fairness of representation is deemed necessary.

For those only interested in soundbites, however, I imagine they will continue to enjoy the mainstream media. For others who may want to hear and digest more, learn much, and make informed opinions from other than bites tailored for a "low information" voter, providing options to hear debate answers in more than severely limited timeframes may be a solution for those who want to glean more from many, so as they become more informed persons they become better prepared persons to cast a vote from knowledge not just bites.

Consider this: on difficult subjects, an answer that is well-thought-out may take up to fifteen minutes, maybe even a half hour, maybe an hour! How many people would want that much information before casting a ballot?

The Lincoln debate settings and speeches between 1858 and 1860, provided audiences information and stories about many of Lincoln's humble beginnings, and his accomplishments were becoming more generally known. But perhaps not as well-known were these lines, composed when he was quite young.

When merely a school boy, Lincoln had written school notes which his stepmother had saved, and had presented to Herndon after Lincoln's death:

> "Abraham Lincoln
> His hand and pen
> He will be good
> But God knows when."

This above is Herndon's punctuation. A photograph of the actual document reads like this, from a book by Stefan Lorant:

Glen Aubrey

"Abraham Lincoln
his hand and pen
he will be good
but god knows When"

We'll forgive the punctuation of a school boy, but I'm inclined to believe that his punctuation was intentional. You may wish to try and locate a photo of his writing. Lincoln's penmanship is exceptionally neat. He was also a smart kid. I believe he meant to say it the way he did.

The processes of acquisition of knowledge, the development of character, along with associations with other people, start early. They should. The words one uses and how they are positioned and communicated are important as is their meaning and intent.

3

Character on Display in Springfield

During February of 2017, in honor of the anniversary of Lincoln's birth (February 12, 1809), I was invited to conduct two book signings of the four Lincoln books I had authored. These book signing events took place at the Visitor's Center, Lincoln Home National Historic Site (U.S. National Park Service) as well as the charming Prairie Archives book store in Springfield, Illinois. It was an honor to be engaged in these opportunities at both locations. Thank you to the leadership and staffs for their graciousness.

The interest in Lincoln history, according to some scholars who were present, seems to have waned. Not mine, however. I still thirst for more knowledge and the reasons behind his leadership.

In preparation for writing and publishing this work, I again visited Springfield on April 12, 2017, primarily to take photos of what is often called Lincoln Square, adjacent to the Old State Capitol Building. On the southeast corner of the square is located the law office which Lincoln shared with William Herndon.

Lincoln Square, Springfield, Illinois, April, 2017
Old State Capitol Building and sculptures of Mary Todd, Lincoln's wife, and Lincoln where Mary is seen adjusting his clothing.

Lincoln and Herndon Law Offices, Springfield, Illinois, April, 2017

Across the street from the old capitol building grounds, facing directly east, one can see the façade of Springfield Marine Bank. When Lincoln resided and worked in Springfield this was the bank he used, beginning in 1853. The history of that bank and Lincoln's association with it are fascinating.

Springfield Marine Bank
April, 2017

Banking is a part of everyday life, of course. Handling money is not optional; how one does so and into whose hands funds are entrusted are choices everyone makes.

Touring the immediate area and visiting with businesses, I was gratified to receive an offer from one helpful employee, to obtain a three-fold flyer about the history of the old bank and Lincoln's association with it. This three-fold flyer is no longer in print and is without a copyright notice. I gratefully accepted this gift from an individual who shall remain anonymous. The front page of the flyer proudly announces: "Abraham Lincoln's bank, the oldest bank in Illinois ... (so far, he's our favorite President/customer."

I learned that a book or pamphlet entitled *The Marine Bank – The Story of the Oldest Bank in Illinois* was written by author Paul M. Angle (b. 1900, d. 1975). The online version lists a copyright date of 1931. According to the University of Illinois Urbana-Champaign, the work is in the Public Domain. "Published 1923-1963 with notice but no evidence of copyright renewal found in Stanford Copyright Renewal Database."

The three-fold flyer content is attributed to the writings of Mr. Angle. "Local attorney Abraham Lincoln maintained an account with the company beginning in 1853." Under the heading of A. Lincoln, Depositor: "On March 1, 1853, a man well known throughout central Illinois as an honest, competent attorney walked into the Springfield Marine and Fire Insurance Company. Mr. Robert Irwin, secretary of the company, was in the large, high-ceilinged banking room behind an open horseshoe-shaped counter, laboriously making pen and ink entries in great leather-bound ledgers. Mr. Irwin proceeded to open an account with the $310 his acquaintance Abraham Lincoln handed him. Across the top of a blank page in Depositor's Ledger B, he wrote, 'A. Lincoln.' From that day until the day of his death, Abraham Lincoln was a customer of the Springfield Marine and Fire Insurance Company."

How do persons of high character and leadership like Abraham Lincoln entrust and use their money? The flyer continues, "When coupled with what we know of Mr. Lincoln's life, his bank account becomes an important historical document. The $310 Lincoln deposited when he opened the account was withdrawn five weeks later. A second deposit of $400 was made October 11, and then withdrawn on November 18." The account was used sparingly until 1859.

"During that year, twenty-five deposits, ranging from $24.75 to $625 were made and eighty-four sums, varying from $1.60 to $505 were withdrawn. This activity level continued throughout 1860 and into 1861, until the Lincolns' departure for Washington."

He lived within his means—a core characteristic of someone who knew how to manage assets. "As an attorney, Lincoln's income from his law practice averaged $3,000 a year, borne out by his account deposits... On this income Lincoln was able to support his family in a fashion consistent with his own national prominence, to keep his oldest son at Phillips Exeter Academy, and still to maintain a running balance of several hundred dollars ..."

In early August, 1857, "...he had collected his largest fee—a sum of $4,800, for which he had brought suit against the Illinois Central Railroad Company. The draft was deposited on August 12, and the entire amount withdrawn on the thirty-first, to be divided between the two law partners, Lincoln and William H [sic] Herndon." He paid what he owed; he was an honest lawyer!

He had to manage money carefully. Campaigning against Douglas "meant thousands of miles of travel, most of the expense borne by the two contestants. Lincoln was compelled to marshal every financial resource, and he himself confessed, after the election, that he was without money even for household expenses."

Men of great character understand owning the responsibilities that accompany risks of attaining higher goals. "When Lincoln left Springfield in February 1861 to assume his Presidential duties in Washington he withdrew $400 and purchased three $100 drafts on the Metropolitan Bank in New York. The years of Lincoln's Presidency show a gradually increasing balance in his account and at the time of his re-election in 1864 it had mounted to more than $4,500."

It is known that his wife, Mary Lincoln, did not share her husband's frugalness or keen financial planning. In fact, she often hid purchases from him and over-spent constantly after the election in 1860.

Her overindulgence was rampant. According to one source, "At one point, she purchased 400 pairs of gloves in a four month period."

Further, "'I must dress in costly materials,' she said to a friend. 'The President glances at my rich dresses and is happy to believe that the few hundred dollars that I obtain from him supply all my wants…if he is elected, I can keep him in ignorance of my affairs, but if he is defeated [in the reelection], then the bills will be sent.'" Her spending continued after their son, Willie, died in 1862, and not unlike many going through a devastating grieving process, she spent great amounts of money in an effort to ease her pain of loss.

Mr. Lincoln found out about her spending, eventually. He was not happy, putting it mildly. "By 1864, her debts had run up to $27,000, nearly a half million dollars of value in 2017 dollars…" "Desperate, she would share political secrets with officials or promise political favors in exchange for loans. She even sold off excess manure purchased to fertilize White House grounds, and fired mansion staff to save money."

After Lincoln's death, "…creditors descended upon the fragile woman. They had previously granted unlimited credit, and now demanded payment. Congress granted her a one-time pension payment of $25,000, but it was not enough to cover her debts or spending habits. She ended up selling many of her personal belongings, and her supporters helped as much as they could. Though she eventually paid off her debts, swirling rumors and the actions she took to secure personal loans ruined her reputation and relationship with many friends."

Portrait of Mary Lincoln from a newspaper clipping dated October 18, 1896. Mrs. Lincoln died in 1882.

President Lincoln was assassinated on April 14, 1865 and died on the morning of April 15. "After his death, David Davis, the administrator of President Lincoln's estate, took charge and on June 16, 1865 closed the account and withdrew the balance of $9,044.41, about one tenth of Lincoln's total personal estate."

At the beginning of his law career, in 1837, Lincoln moved to Springfield. There he met Mary Todd, and the couple married in 1842. They purchased their house in 1844. It is located at 413 S. 8th Street (the corner of 8th and Jackson Streets). The Lincoln Home Visitor Center is located at 426 S. 7th Street. Only pedestrian traffic is permitted between the Visitor's Center and the Lincoln home.

Touring the historic home today, visitors are told that this home was the only home that Lincoln ever owned. During the time he lived in Springfield, Lincoln was elected to the House of Representatives in 1846. Upon his election as President in 1860, the Lincoln family moved to the White House in Washington, D.C. (then known as Washington City).

The Lincoln Home, Springfield, Illinois, April, 2017

August 8, 1860: A Great Republican Rally in front of the Lincoln's home in Springfield, Illinois, following his nomination in 1860. Lincoln can be seen just to the right of the main doorway in the middle of the home. He is wearing a light colored jacket. He also is taller than everyone else!

Lincoln Sculpture, Lincoln Plaza, Springfield, Illinois, April, 2017

4

Who Was Mary Todd and What Was Her Influence on Lincoln?

It is generally concluded that at one point Mr. Lincoln may have told his wife, the former Mary Todd, that she could be committed to an asylum if she could not control her grief after their son, Willie, had died. Willie was eleven years old when he passed away on February 20, 1862 in the White House.

> For further study, please see: https://www.quora.com/Did-Abe-Lincoln-really-threaten-Mary-with-the-madhouse-when-Will-died-as-the-movie-stated.

It is also known that Robert Lincoln, the eldest son of Abraham and Mary, had his mother committed to an asylum in 1875.

> Please see https://en.wikipedia.org/wiki/Mary_Todd_Lincoln.

William Herndon employed colorful language to describe the Lincolns, especially when referencing Mary. Writing about the young Mary Todd, Herndon wrote, "She was of the average height, weighing when I first saw her about a hundred and thirty pounds. She was rather compactly built, had a well rounded [sic] face, rich dark-brown hair, and bluish-gray eyes. In her bearing she was proud, but handsome and vivacious. Her education had been in no wise defective; she was a good conversationalist, using with equal fluency the French and English languages. When she used a pen, its point was sure to be sharp, and she wrote with wit and ability. She not only had a quick intellect but an intuitive judgment of men and their motives. Ordinarily she was affable and even charming in her manners; but when offended or antagonized, her agreeable qualities instantly disappeared beneath a wave of stinging satire or sarcastic bitterness, and her entire better nature was submerged. In her figure and physical proportions, in education, bearing, temperament, history — in everything she was the exact reverse of Lincoln."

We are told that while opposites attract, they also repel. The makeup of the Lincoln's courtship, marriage, family, and eventual national prominence would be subject to many ups, downs, severe disappointments, and great elation. This was much to thrust upon a young couple who already was in the public eye to a large degree long before the election of 1860. Was it too much for this youthful couple to embrace and endure?

Herndon at one point quotes a Mrs. Harriet Chapman, a lady relative who lived with Lincoln and his wife for two years after their marriage. She stated on November 8, 1887,

"...she loved Douglas [Steven Douglas], and but for her promise to marry Lincoln would have accepted him." This would not demonstrate a stable and enduring commitment. In fact, on their wedding date, January 1, 1841, Lincoln never showed up, according to Herndon—an account disputed by Lorant, who called Herndon's account, "entirely untrue." However, Herndon's description of what followed is this: "What the feelings of a lady as sensitive, passionate, and proud as Miss Todd were we can only imagine—no one can ever describe them." By the next morning, "after persistent search, Lincoln's friends found him. Restless, gloomy, miserable, desperate, he seemed an object of pity. His friends, [Joshua] Speed among the number fearing a tragic termination, watched him closely in their rooms day and night. 'Knives and razors, and every instrument that could be used for self-destruction were removed from his reach.' Mrs. Edwards [in whose home the wedding ceremony was to have taken place] did not hestitate [sic] to regard him as insane, and of course her sister Mary shared in that view. But the case was hardly so desperate. His condition began to improve after a few weeks, and a letter written to his law partner Stuart, on the 23rd of January, 1841, reveals more perfectly how he felt. He says, 'I am now the most miserable man living. If what I feel were equally distributed to the whole human family, there would not be one cheerful face on earth. Whether I shall ever be better, I cannot tell; I awfully forebode I shall not. To remain as I am is impossible. I must die or be better, as it appears to me ... I fear I shall be unable to attend to any business here, and a change of scene might help me. If I could be myself I would rather remain at home with Judge Logan. I can write no more.'"

Lincoln's acquaintances at this time brought him great assistance. Joshua Speed, who was a dear friend of Lincoln and who appeared to care with counsel, understanding, and advice, invited Lincoln to go to live with Speed's parents near Louisville, Kentucky in what Herndon noted was "a magnificent place." Lincoln went. Herndon: "Speed's mother was much impressed with the tall and swarthy stranger her son had brought with him. She was a God-fearing mother, and besides aiding to lighten his spirits, gave him a Bible, advising him to read it and by adopting its precepts obtain a release from his troubles which no other agency, in her judgment, could bring him." A letter from Joshua Speed dated February 6, 1866 regarding this time of Lincoln's life stated, "He [Lincoln] was much depressed. At first he almost contemplated suicide. In the deepest of his depression he said one day he had done nothing to make any human being remember that he had lived; and that to connect his name with the events transpiring in his day and generation, and so impress himself upon them as to link his name with something that would redound to the interest of his fellow-men, was what he desired to live for."

Through times of severe disappointment, his motivation and sense of renewal were returning, apparently, and so was his aspiration for achievement. Indeed it could be ascertained that his desire to "make something of himself" made a large contribution toward rebounding health and vitality.

Receiving the gift of the Bible must have helped, too. Lincoln had been gratified to receive it from Mrs. Speed. Many years later, on October 3, 1861, as president, he signed a photograph of himself to her stating, "For Mrs. Lucy G. Speed, from whose pious hand I accepted the present of an Oxford Bible twenty years ago." He recalled that memorable event for which he was grateful amid the early and extremely frustrating beginnings of the Civil War.

Lincoln's renewal was evidenced on several fronts. Quoted by Herndon in a letter to Joshua Speed, July 4 of the same year following Speed's marriage to his wife, Fanny, Lincoln wrote, "I must gain confidence in my own ability to keep my resolves when they are made. In that ability I once prided myself as the only chief gem of my character; that gem I lost, how and where you know too well. I have not regained it; and until I do I cannot trust myself in any matter of much importance." He continued, "… I always was superstitious, I believe God made me one of the instruments of bringing Fanny and you together, which union I have no doubt he had foreordained. Whatever he designs he will do for me yet. 'Stand still and see the salvation of the Lord,' is my text just now."

Quoting scripture appeared easy for Lincoln. He did it a lot before being elected to national office and while serving as president. He must have known the contents of his Bible well.

Observe Lincoln's curious and heartfelt questioning in another letter to Speed on October 5, 1842 asking about the marriage, quoted by Herndon: "'But I want to ask a close question: "Are you in *feeling* as well as *judgment* glad you are married as you are?" From anybody but me this would be an impudent question, not to be tolerated, but I know you will pardon it in me. Please answer it quickly, as I am impatient to know.'"

Herndon relates the renewed courtship and marriage. "It is unnecessary to prolong the account of this strange and checkered courtship."

"One morning in November, Lincoln hastening to the room of his friend James H. Matheney before the latter had arisen from bed, informed that he was to be married that night, and requested him to attend as best man. That same morning Miss Todd called on her friend Julia M. Jayne, who afterward married Lyman Trumbull, and made a similar request. The Edwardses [sic] were notified, and made such meager preparation as were possible on so short notice. License was obtained during the day, the minister, Charles N. Dresser, was sent for, and in the evening of November 4, 1842, 'as pale and trembling as if being driven to slaughter,' Abraham Lincoln was at last married to Mary Todd."

Here is Herndon's analysis, which can hardly be seen in isolation; rather, it emerges from years of observance and interchange. Recalling this time of Lincoln's early life, Herndon wrote: "One great trial of his life was now over, and another still greater one was yet to come. To me it has always seemed plain that Mr. Lincoln married Mary Todd to save his honor, and in doing that he sacrificed his domestic peace. He had searched himself subjectively, introspectively, thoroughly; he knew he did not love her, but he had promised to marry her! The hideous thought came up like a nightmare. As the 'fatal first of January, 1841', neared, the clouds around him blackened the heavens and his life almost went out with the storm. But soon the skies cleared. Friends interposed their aid to avert a calamity, and at last he stood face to face with the great conflict between honor and domestic peace. He chose the former, and with it years of self-torture, sacrificial pangs, and the loss forever of a happy home.

"With Miss Todd a different motive, but one equally as unfortunate, prompted her adherence to the union. To marry Lincoln meant not a life of luxury and ease, for Lincoln was not a man to accumulate wealth; but in him she saw position in society, prominence in the world, and the grandest social distinction. By that means her ambition would be satisfied. Until that fatal New Year's day [sic] in 1841 she may have loved him, but his action on that occasion forfeited her affection. He had crushed her proud, womanly spirit. She felt degraded in the eyes of the world. Love fled at the approach of revenge. Some writer—it is Junius, I believe—as said that, 'Injuries may be forgiven and forgotten, but insults admit of no compensation; they degrade the mind in its own self-esteem and force it to recover its level by revenge.' Whether Mrs. Lincoln really was moved by the spirit of revenge or not she acted along the lines of human conduct. She led her husband a wild and merry dance. If in time, she became soured at the world it was not without provocation, and if in later years she unchained the bitterness of a disappointed and outraged nature, it followed as logically as an effect does the cause.

"I have told this sad story as I know and have learned it."

5

Early Marriage, Financial Hardships, Home Life

The newly married couple boarded at the Globe Tavern in Springfield and Herndon describes these days as fiscally hard. "Gaining a livelihood was slow and discouraging business with him, for we find him in another letter apologizing for his failure to visit Kentucky, 'because,' he says, 'I am so poor and make so little headway in the world that I drop back in a month of idleness as much as I gain in a year's sowing.'"

Many of us, author included, have faced financial difficulties, sometimes severe and daunting. Not in any way unique to a single situation, the recession beginning in 2007-2008 cost up to 40% of personal wealth for the average American. Throughout the Obama administration the recession lingered and with it so many devastating effects that many people have yet to regain lost ground. Several sectors of the economy were hit particularly hard. From personal experience and knowledge from friends and associates, losses continued to mount and in some cases were never abated apart from bankruptcy.

The *Washington Post* claimed this figure of a 40% loss from the years 2007-2010.
> https://www.washingtonpost.com/business/economy/fed-americans-wealth-dropped-40-percent/2012/06/11/gJQAlIsCVV_story.html

How do you handle fiscal disappointment? One of the first items that companies deemed it necessary to "drop" when the recession hit, was team building and team training consultation. What a shame … just when they needed it the most.

How a person, regardless of personality, faces tough times is a reflection of beliefs and character. Clearly some perform worse and some better than others.

It is in tough economic times when heart core truths and beliefs shine through. Many years before the recession of the new millennium, when my father had his business in San Diego and other locations during the 60s and 70s, a local competitor of his suffered a major loss due to fire and flood at a warehouse. My father and I talked about it and he considered what if anything should or could be done. I will ever remember the lesson my dad taught me through his example. He extended a helping hand to the competitor, offering him product in order to keep him in business so he could literally survive. I know: I delivered much of the product. No one told my dad to do it; that action emerged as part of who he was. He had been a young man in the Great Depression, he had survived, later built a business and became successful through hard, very hard work. And long hours. Forty years' worth. Yes, that was a different era than the one in which we currently live, but character like that shines through regardless of the generation, the label, the circumstances.

Since that time of assisting the competitor, who by the way did survive, "helping" when possible became a trait embraced by many who knew my dad. I clearly was impressed and learned the lesson, and have since used it.

I was known to tell this story in consulting seminars, and audience reactions were nearly always ones of quiet amazement. Shouldn't caring actions like this be commonplace?

In 2017, the southern parts of Texas in and around Houston were ravaged by Hurricane Harvey. Texas governor, Greg Abbott, was seen on television programs during and after the crisis, stating words to this effect: that this was the time when Texans helped each other and provided assistance to those people who needed it. Indeed, remarkable stories of rescue and survival emerged from these tragedies along with thousands who volunteered their time, energy, money and more to help victims of the storms.

These were heartwarming tales and said much of the culture of this great state.

Of course, bad apples were present, too: looters and selfish merchants who revealed their greed by trying to take advantage of those who were suffering. Poor choices became readily seen from businesses that could have cared less and spiked prices while they thought they might have the chance.

Unfortunately, many banks fall into this greed category, too, when in difficult times like a recession, they appear to be more interested in profits than people. Their greed apparently knows no boundaries and their "take all that is possible to take" attitudes and actions in crises don't or may not change when times get better. But their customers remember. And they should.

In stark contrast stands any institution that not only gives, but gives more than is needed to assist because they want to, not necessarily because they have to. How refreshing.

Have you ever been the beneficiary of an organization or entity that cared more about you the person than you the disadvantaged customer, regardless of the source of difficulty? Have you ever been the one who gives, not trumpeting your giving, but just gives whether anyone notices or not, because it is part of your character?

Lincoln's character as a person was one of determination in hard times; it meant hard work, going above and beyond in efforts to achieve. Do you believe that sometimes great loss is character's gain? Lincoln was no stranger to loss; history was to prove that over and over in his ascension to power and presidency. The Civil War was loss personified; most estimates put the human sacrifice at 600,000 lives in both North and South.

Perhaps his thoughts about such horrible devastation within the Civil War, as well as the tragedies that were parts of his family before and during his White House years, were seen in the immensity in his Second Inaugural Address March 4, 1865, a masterpiece. He concluded with these words:

> *With malice toward none, with charity for all, with firmness in the right as God gives us to see the right, let us strive on to finish the work we are in, to bind up the nation's wounds, to care for him who shall have borne the battle and for his widow and his orphan, to do all which may achieve and cherish a just and lasting peace among ourselves and with all nations.*

To the credit of his wife, in their early days at Springfield, at least according to Herndon, she shared in his sacrifices. We may be interested to know what she brought to the marriage and how she influenced Lincoln. Herndon: "She was gifted with a rare insight into the motives that actuate mankind, and there is no doubt that much of Lincoln's success was in a measure attributable to her acuteness and the stimulus of her influence." These words are in sharp contrast to Herndon's prior lines on their marriage. He continued, "She loved power and prominence, and when occasionally she came down to our office, it seemed to me then that she was inordinately proud of her tall and ungainly husband. She saw in him bright prospects ahead, and his every move was watched by her with the closest interest."

Herndon relates that he spent about one fourth of the time with Lincoln when Lincoln was "riding the circuit" which was "over half the year." During these law trips on the circuit, "he studied Euclid until he could with ease demonstrate all the propositions in the six books." What a mind he had!

By any standard, Lincoln was away from home a lot. Consider these lines: "On Saturdays the court and attorneys, if within a reasonable distance, would usually start for their homes. Some went for a fresh supply of clothing, but the greater number went simply to spend a day of rest with their families. The only exception was Lincoln, who usually spent his Sundays with the loungers at the country tavern, and only went home at the end of the circuit or term of court. 'At first,' relates one of his colleagues on the circuit, 'we wondered at it, but soon learned to account for his strange disinclination to go home. Lincoln himself never had much to say about home, and we never felt free to comment on it. Most of us had pleasant, inviting homes, and as we struck out for them I'm sure each one of us down in our hearts had a mingled feeling of pity and sympathy for him.'"

"Melancholy" is generally described as dejection, a pensive mood, or depression, whether clinical or not. Lincoln has been characterized as melancholy in his mannerism and personality. Herndon did say at one point, "His melancholy dripped from him as he walked." An excellent article on this and related items can be accessed at https://www.theatlantic.com/magazine/archive/2005/10/lincolns-great-depression/304247/. None of us were there so it is difficult to form an independent opinion; and there are many whose thoughts have contributed to the discussion.

The point here: what was it about "going home" that was not on Lincoln's priority list? Personal values and judgments come into play. We learn that during these times of being away from family, perhaps lonely or depressed, it was not uncommon for Lincoln to engage whoever would listen in storytelling, and he was good at it. When Lincoln would engage in a story, "…his melancholy, taking to itself wings, seemed to fly away." Some would call this an escape, a coping mechanism.

Regardless, quoting Herndon who possessed firsthand experience with Lincoln's storytelling abilities, we read: "In the role of a story-teller [sic] I am prone to regard Mr. Lincoln as without an equal. I have seen him surrounded by a crowd numbering as many as two and in some cases three hundred persons, all deeply interested in the outcome of a story which, when he had finished it, speedily found repetition in every grocery and lounging place within reach. His power of mimicry ... and his manner of recital, were in many respects unique, if not remarkable. His countenance and all his features seemed to take part in the performance."

During the Civil War, his storytelling was criticized by some while others were entertained. When so many were dying and the devastation was so awful, Lincoln said at one point, answering the criticism, "If I couldn't tell these stories, I would die." You may want to review this website for some of his stories, and read a superb article about his use of stories and humor, a tactic which he used often.
http://www.saturdayeveningpost.com/2010/03/27/history/post-perspective/lincoln-laughter.html.

Why did he tell stories? To laugh, to entertain, make a point, to survive, to communicate, and more. Lincoln was witty, quick, and he knew how to talk to the common man — because he was one — although exceptionally smart. His person, and personality under control, combined to help him survive in the most agonizing of times.

He expounded great truths, moral absolutes, and often engaged in humor in his storytelling. There were priceless moments of real-life application that came from his mouth. One of my favorite examples of Lincoln's quick wit which I've memorized from reading it 50 years ago and quoted many times in seminars, was this: Abraham Lincoln once ran for Congress against pioneer preacher, Peter Cartwright. At one time Mr. Lincoln attended one of Cartwright's sermons. Mr. Cartwright asked everybody who wished to go to heaven to stand up. Almost everyone stood. Then he asked everybody who did not want to go to hell to stand up. At this point, everybody but Mr. Lincoln was standing. Mr. Cartwright then said, "I observe that many of you accepted my invitation to give their hearts to God and go to heaven. I further observed that all but one of you indicated an aversion to going to hell. The sole exception is Mr. Lincoln, who failed to respond to either invitation. May I inquire of you, Mr. Lincoln, where you are going?" Mr. Lincoln replied, "I'm going to Congress." Classic.

Melancholy, humorous, witty, entertaining ... crowds enjoyed what he had to say and apparently melancholy became subject to his storytelling. There was no option for Mr. Lincoln to be a public figure. It was his destiny — at least it became one. His storytelling was part of it.

How about his family? As we understand, he was absent on the circuit much of the time when he, Mary, and his sons lived in Springfield, Illinois. What was it about his home life that Lincoln allowed to be reasons for not returning home when he could have?

Perhaps Herndon throws some light on this subject, but reading his remarks must be accomplished with an understanding that while he claims he wanted to be accurate and fair (author's description) he clearly manifests a dislike for Mrs. Lincoln and her influence on Mr. Lincoln.

Consider this passage where Herndon appears to excuse himself for revealing facts about Lincoln's person and home life: "…I am revealing an element of his character that has heretofore been kept from the world; but in doing so I feel sure I am treading on no person's toes, for all the actors in this domestic drama are dead, and the world seems ready to hear the facts."

Mary Lincoln had a temper—this we have learned. "…one of her greatest misfortunes was her inability to control her temper. Admit that, and everything can be explained." Apparently Lincoln was "meek and mild" when it came to home or domestic matters, though he was firm, forceful, entertaining, and "impressive" as Herndon alludes, in public dealings. Herndon quoting Judge David Davis: "…as a general rule, when all the lawyers of a Saturday evening would go home and see their families and friends, Lincoln would find some excuse and refuse to go. We said nothing, but it seemed to us all he was not domestically happy." The loneliness must have been deep, though he was surrounded by crowds on many occasions.

Lincoln and his wife had four boys.
- Robert Todd Lincoln, their firstborn son was born August 1, 1843, in Springfield, Illinois, and died July 26, 1926 in Manchester, Vermont. Age 83.
- Edward Baker Lincoln was their second son. "Eddie" was used as a nickname and the name is on his gravestone in Springfield, Illinois. He was born March 10, 1846 in Springfield and died February 1, 1850 in Springfield. Age 4.
- William Wallace Lincoln, "Willie" was the third son. He was born December 21, 1850 in Springfield, and died February 20, 1862 at the White House. Age 12.
- Thomas "Tad" Lincoln was their fourth son, and the youngest. He was born April 4, 1853 in Springfield and died July 15, 1871 in Chicago, Illinois. Age 18. Mr. Lincoln provided his nickname, describing the little guy "as wiggly as a tadpole."

Herndon, referring to Lincoln's parenting, stated, "He exercised no government of any kind over his household. His children did much as they pleased. Many of their antics he approved, and he restrained them in nothing. He never reproved them or gave them a fatherly frown. He was the most indulgent parent I have ever known."

Lincoln would bring Willie and Tad to the office on Sundays while his wife attended church. "He seldom accompanied her there." And the boys made havoc of the office, according to Herndon, and Lincoln was permissive.

Their home life was punctuated with Mary Lincoln's frequent rage over simple things, like which butter knife to use and whether to send a servant to answer the door (which Lincoln often answered himself). Mary Lincoln and Abraham Lincoln were completely unique from one another: one highly refined, polished, for whom "image" and "bearing" were apparent determiners of value, and the other homespun and some would even say crude by comparison. "Her frequent outbursts of temper precipitated many an embarrassment from which Lincoln with great difficulty extricated himself."

Mr. Lincoln even was known to secretly pay one household lady servant an extra dollar per week "on condition that she [the servant] would brave whatever storms might arise, and suffer whatever might befall her, without complaint."

A male visitor once came to the house to ask Mrs. Lincoln why she had unceremoniously dismissed the man's niece from employment. This man became a victim of one of Mary Lincoln's tirades. He retreated and went to see Lincoln as Herndon noted, "...determined to exact from him proper satisfaction for his wife's action." After Lincoln heard his tale, he said, "My friend, I regret to hear this, but let me ask you in all candor, can't you endure for a few moments what I have had as my daily portion for the last fifteen years?" According to Herndon, "These words were spoken so mournfully and with such a look of distress that the man was completely disarmed." Apparently they became good friends, as well.

Lincoln was an adherent to a belief of fatalism during the times that people like Herndon were close to him. Mary Lincoln had said to Herndon after Mr. Lincoln's death that "his only philosophy was, what is to be will be, and no prayers of ours can reverse the degree." Herndon: "He always contended that he was doomed to a sad fate, and he repeatedly said to me when we were alone in our office: 'I am sure I shall meet with some terrible end.'"

One of Lincoln's favorite poems was this one, *Mortality*, written in 1824 by William Knox. Lincoln knew it by heart. It is quoted here verbatim:

Mortality

O why should the spirit of mortal be proud!
Like a fast flitting meteor, a fast flying cloud,
A flash of the lightning, a break of the wave —
He passes from life to his rest in the grave.
The leaves of the oak and the willows shall fade,
Be scattered around, and together be laid;
And the young and the old, and the low and the high,
Shall moulder to dust, and together shall lie.
The child that a mother attended and loved,
The mother that infant's affection that proved,
The husband that mother and infant that blest,

Glen Aubrey

Each — all are away to their dwelling of rest.
The maid on whose cheek, on whose brow, in whose eye,
Shone beauty and pleasure — her triumphs are by:
And the memory of those that beloved her and praised,
Are alike from the minds of the living erased.
The hand of the king that the sceptre hath borne,
The brow of the priest that the mitre hath worn,
The eye of the sage, and the heart of the brave,
Are hidden and lost in the depths of the grave.
The peasant whose lot was to sow and to reap,
The herdsman who climbed with his goats to the steep,
The beggar that wandered in search of his bread,
Have faded away like the grass that we tread.
The saint that enjoyed the communion of Heaven,
The sinner that dared to remain unforgiven,
The wise and the foolish, the guilty and just,
Have quietly mingled their bones in the dust.
So the multitude goes — like the flower and the weed
That wither away to let others succeed;
So the multitude comes — even those we behold,
To repeat every tale that hath often been told.
For we are the same things that our fathers have been,
We see the same sights that our fathers have seen,
We drink the same stream, and we feel the same sun,
And we run the same course that our fathers have run.

The thoughts we are thinking our fathers would think,
From the death we are shrinking from they too would shrink,
To the life we are clinging to they too would cling —
But it speeds from the earth like a bird on the wing.
They loved — but their story we cannot unfold;
They scorned — but the heart of the haughty is cold;
They grieved — but no wail from their slumbers may come;
They joyed — but the voice of their gladness is dumb.
They died — ay, they died! and we, things that are now,
Who walk on the turf that lies over their brow,
Who make in their dwellings a transient abode,
Meet the change they met on their pilgrimage road.
Yea, hope and despondence, and pleasure and pain,
Are mingled together like sunshine and rain;
And the smile and the tear, and the song and the dirge,
Still follow each other like surge upon surge.
Tis the twink of an eye, 'tis the draught of a breath,
From the blossom of health to the paleness of death,
From the gilded saloon to the bier and the shroud —
O why should the spirit of mortal be proud!

These lines, to the degree Lincoln identified with them, may speak much about his view of life and death. This poem reminds many of the Book of Ecclesiastes with its "meaningless!" and "under the sun" positions of futility, or of the story of Job where nothing Job could do could change the reality of devastating loss, and he was sorely tempted to reject his God. At the end of the Book of Job, it is recorded that God and Job have a conversation about who is in charge—it became clear in the conversation that God is. Eventually Job becomes blessed because of his trust in God—he didn't follow his wife's advice to curse God and die, and his family and wealth were restored. Not really futility after all.

Many people see a different "faith" paradigm in Lincoln's Second Inaugural Address, where clearly quoted passages from the Bible are paramount and used as guiding principles. This speech was given about a month before his assassination.

Herndon quotes Jesse W. Fell to whom Lincoln first confided the details of his biography and who "furnishes a more elaborate account of the [Lincoln's] religious views than anyone else." Fell says this about Lincoln's religion: "…his principles and practices and the spirit of his whole life were of the very kind we universally agree to call Christian; and I think this conclusion is in no wise affected by the circumstance that he never attached himself to any religious society whatever."

Further, "His religious views were eminently practical, and are summed up, as I think, in these two propositions: the Fatherhood of God, and the brotherhood of man. He fully believed in a superintending and overruling Providence that guides and controls the operations of the world, but maintained that law and order, and not their violation or suspension, are the appointed means by which this Providence is exercised."

Herndon even quotes Mrs. Lincoln on the subject of religious faith. "Mr. Lincoln had no faith and no hope in the usual acceptation of those words. He never joined a Church; but still, as I believe, he was a religious man by nature. He first seemed to think about the subject when our boy Willie died, and then more than ever about the time he went to Gettysburg; but it was a kind of poetry in his nature, and he was never a technical Christian."

Herndon concludes: "…he believed in God and immortality; and even if he questioned the existence of future eternal punishment he hoped to find a rest from trouble and a heaven beyond the grave. If at any time in his life he was skeptical of the divine origin or the Bible he ought not for that reason to be condemned; for he accepted the practical precepts of that great book as binding alike upon his head and conscience. The benevolence of his impulses, the seriousness of his convictions, and the nobility of his character are evidences unimpeachable that his soul was ever filled with the exalted purity and sublime faith of natural religion."

Here is what we observe and learn from multiple sources: in his youth, Lincoln was a backwoodsman, roughhewn like many of his countrymen. Lincoln the young man expressed doubt and disbelief in religion. Stories are told of his early inclinations to reject Biblical truth and even deride, ridicule, and argue against doctrines and practices based on the Bible. He claimed he was a fatalist. He married a woman possibly not for love (according to Herndon) but to regain his honor; he contemplated suicide after not showing up for his wedding, but seemed to recover. If this is a part of the definition of a melancholy personality, the description fits. Yet he was an upstanding, well-known, and respected businessman in Springfield. He conducted a professional lawyer's life where going home was not a priority, was highly permissive with this children's behavior (in the White House, too), and endured the rantings of a wife who eventually was committed to an asylum by their son. Mary was a wife who exhibited an uncontrolled temper in and around the home and within their networks; yet in spite of the negative environments which he endured, Lincoln sought to exercise kindness to the common man; he told the truth, was a gifted and brilliant lawyer, a shrewd but honest politician. He and his wife experienced tragic family deaths of two children. He was an eloquent speaker who in his later speeches indicated a growing dependence on God in whom he had always believed. He loved telling stories to lighten a moment of crisis, or for their entertainment value. As history proved, he led this country in its most tumultuous time. He was elected to the presidency twice, eventually losing his life to an assassin's bullet one month into his second term.

What do you think it would take for someone of such complexity to ascend to the highest office of leadership in the land who, upon being elected, was to endure the most costly war in human sacrifice the world had ever known?

How does a leader in the making endure extreme variances of existence like these? What kind of person could experience and grow through these? Some would state that his life journeys, including his marriage, prepared him for the leadership task to which he was eventually elected. Predestined? Foreordained? What made Lincoln endure?

The strength we observe of character, honor, tolerance, and dedication to just causes is admirable and exemplary. Think about these great goals, a few of many: being committed to high and lofty ideals and beliefs no matter the costly sacrifice, believing unreservedly in the perpetuity of the Union, emancipating the slaves "as a war measure" to benefit the Union, deeply resolute on restoring the Union after the war, as well as earnestly desiring and working for a vote to approve and ratify the 13th Amendment to abolish slavery for all time. These lofty causes needed, even required the leadership he provided, even though his life was cut short before fully seeing the final results for which he had worked so hard.

Storied truths in antiquity ring true: for such a time as this someone was prepared and rose to fulfill his (or her) destiny for the cause of the greater good. I am sure Lincoln had read this scripture; remember, he knew his Bible well. Esther 4:14b (Authorized King James Version of 1611) "... and who knoweth whether thou art come to the kingdom for such a time as this?"

6
Ambition

No one accomplishes anything of merit by wishing and dreaming alone. Action and hard work, born of a steadfast desire to succeed and overcome obstacles must accompany desire, hope, aspiration, and dependence on God; for then only will achievements come.

Ward H. Lamon knew Lincoln well, though not for as long as did Herndon. Lamon played vital roles in Lincoln's presidency. Lamon was a self-appointed personal bodyguard for Lincoln, though Lincoln had invited Lamon to accompany him to Washington after Lincoln's first election.* According to Stefan Lorant, it was Lamon who introduced Lincoln at Gettysburg for Lincoln's delivery of the Gettysburg Address.

*https://en.wikipedia.org/wiki/Ward_Hill_Lamon

Note the following tie-in to William Herndon. These two men had close association with Lincoln and shared multiple-year experiences with him, both before and during his presidency.

From the Preface to Lamon's biography: "In the following pages I have endeavored to give the life of Abraham Lincoln, from his birth to his inauguration as President of the United States… At the time of Mr. Lincoln's death, I determined to write his history, as I had in my possession much valuable material for such a purpose. I did not then imagine that any person could have better or more extensive materials than I possessed. I soon learned, however, that Mr. William H. Herndon of Springfield, Ill., was similarly engaged. There could be no rivalry between us; for the supreme object of both was to make the real history and character of Mr. Lincoln as well known to the public as they were to us. He deplored, as I did, the many publications pretending to be biographies which came teeming from the press, so long as the public interest about Mr. Lincoln excited the hope of gain. Out of the mass of works which appeared, of one only—Dr. Holland's—is it possible to speak with any degree of respect.

"Early in 1869, Mr. Herndon placed at my disposal his remarkable collection of materials,—the richest, rarest, and fullest collection it was possible to conceive. Along with them came an offer of hearty co-operation [sic], of which I have availed myself so extensively, that no art of mine would serve to conceal it. Added to my own collections, these acquisitions have enabled me to do what could not have been done before,—prepare an authentic biography of Mr. Lincoln.

"Mr. Herndon had been the partner in business and the intimate personal associate of Mr. Lincoln for something like a quarter of a century; and Mr. Lincoln had lived familiarly with several members of his family long before their individual acquaintance began. New Salem, Springfield, the old judicial circuit, the habits and friends of Mr. Lincoln, were as well known to Mr. Herndon as to himself. With these advantages, and from the numberless facts and hints which had dropped from Mr. Lincoln during the confidential intercourse of an ordinary lifetime, Mr. Herndon was able to institute a thorough system of inquiry for every noteworthy circumstance and every incident of value in Mr. Lincoln's career.

"The fruits of Mr. Herndon's labors are garnered in three enormous volumes of original manuscripts and a mass of unarranged letters and papers. They comprise the recollections of Mr. Lincoln's nearest friends; of the surviving members of his family and his family-connections [sic]; of his schoolfellows, neighbors, and acquaintances in Indiana; of the better part of the whole population of New Salem; of his associates and relatives at Springfield; and of lawyers, judges, politicians, and statesmen everywhere, who had any thing [sic] of interest or moment to relate. They were collected at vast expense of time, labor, and money, involving the employment of many agents, long journeys, tedious examinations, and voluminous correspondence. Upon the value of these materials it would be impossible to place an estimate. That I have used them conscientiously and justly is the only merit to which I lay claim."

Lamon wrote the following from Washington City (Washington, D.C.) in May, 1872. He was recalling Lincoln's farewell to his beloved Springfield, Illinois in 1860 as he embarked to Washington City to fulfill his new role as president.

Lamon quoted Lincoln's farewell speech delivered one day before his birthday, February 11, 1861, exactly as you see it below. The weather was a "drizzling" rain, which likely matched many of the emotions of the people present, including Lincoln. Observe the pathos and gut-wrenching honesty of the person who uttered these words addressed to those who knew him best for more than twenty-five years:

> "Friends, No one who has never been placed in a like position can understand my feelings at this hour, nor the oppressive sadness I feel at this parting. For more than a quarter of a century I have lived among you, and during all that time I have received nothing but kindness at your hands. Here I have lived from my youth until now I am an old man. Here the most sacred ties of earth were assumed. Here all my children were born; and here one of them lies buried. To you, dear friends, I owe all that I have, all that I am.

All the strange, checkered past seems to crowd now upon my mind. [Lamon's italics] To-day [sic] I leave you. I go to assume a task more difficult than that which devolved upon Washington. Unless the great God, who assisted him, shall be with and aid me, I must fail; but if the same omniscient mind and almighty arm that directed and protected him shall guide and support me, I shall not fail,—I shall succeed. Let us all pray that the God of our fathers may not forsake us now. To him I commend you all. Permit me to ask, that, with equal security and faith, you will invoke his wisdom and guidance for me. With these few words I must leave you: for how long I know not. Friends, one and all, I must now bid you an affectionate farewell."

Herndon and Lamon quoted the same version of the speech; however, Herndon footnotes this: "I was not present when Mr. Lincoln delivered his farewell at the depot at Springfield, and never heard what he said. I have adopted the version of his speech as published in our papers. There has been some controversy over the exact language he used on that occasion, and Mr. Nicolay [one of Lincoln's secretaries] has recently published the speech from what he says is the original MS [manuscript], partly in his own and partly in the handwriting of Mr. Lincoln. Substantially, however, it is like the speech as reproduced here from the Springfield paper."

Lorant quotes the speech differently, accompanied by this explanation (page 109) which includes a photograph of the original manuscript: "After Lincoln finished speaking, the train moved out of the station. The journalist Henry Villard walked into the President-elect's car, asking him for a copy of the address. Lincoln had none, but he was ready to write out the speech for Villard. He took paper and pencil and started to reconstruct what he had said, improving on the sentences as he went along. As the train rocked too hard, John Nicolay, his secretary, took over and continued with the writing, scrawling the words as Lincoln said them."

Note the subtle yet important differences. This Nicolay version is undoubtedly more "Lincolnesque" and is the version most people recognize and remember today. It helped to have this version come from Lincoln's own mouth.

> "No one, not in my situation can appreciate my feeling of sadness at this parting. To this place, and the kindness of these people, I owe everything. Here I have lived a quarter of a century, and have passed from a young to an old man. Here my children have been born, and one is buried. I now leave, not knowing when or whether ever I may return, with a task before me greater than that which rested upon

Washington. Without the assistance of that Divine Being who ever attended him, I cannot succeed. With that assistance I cannot fail. Trusting in Him who can go with me, and remain with you, and be everywhere for good, let us confidently hope that all will yet be well. To His care commending you, as I hope in your prayers you will commend me, I bid you an affectionate farewell."

Lamon quotes the editor of "The Journal": "We have known Mr. Lincoln for many years; we have heard him speak upon a hundred different occasions; but we never saw him so profoundly affected, nor did he ever utter an address which seemed to us so full of simple and touching eloquence, so exactly adapted to the occasion, so worthy of the man and the hour."

This is the heart of the matter: a deepening kind of honest emotion was expressed by the man who remembered and recognized his personal and professional history, his "checkered past" if the newspaper got it right, who valued his family and neighborly relationships, embraced his sorrow and often demonstrated it through personality traits, who was committed to fulfilling his duty, demonstrated strong ambition and determination, and understood the immense weight of responsibility that he was undertaking. He also realized his limits, and publicly articulated his dependence upon God, stating that failure would accompany him without God, and that success would be won if God was with him.

Leaders demonstrate wisdom when their true humility shines forth as Lincoln's did on this public occasion. They are even wiser when their public proclamations mirror their private beliefs and experiences.

So how does ambition work? Certainly it means confronting and overcoming obstacles that cause disruption and concerns, believing in a cause so much that one is willing to sacrifice to achieve the ultimate goal.

One of the great privileges of my life was writing a book with my good friend, Harry Stadille, late in 2012. Harry died in early 2016 and this loss was monumental to many, me among them. Parts of our book spoke directly about ambition, belief, confidence, very hard work, and not giving up — not even thinking about giving up — when times and circumstances became what appeared to be major challenges. Here is a story from the book that serves to illustrate ambition, loss, and eventual victory.

> In 1967, a young man began to compete in forensics, or competitive speech. He started when he was 15, just entering high school. This teenager had already demonstrated remarkable ability to move a crowd when he spoke — he was one of two speakers at his 8th grade graduation. As his Junior High school

education came to a close he was encouraged to meet the speech coach of his high school upon entry, so he did.

The young man joined the speech team. In his initial statewide tournament he came home with two championship first place trophies. Remember, he was 15. Tournaments occurred on weekends, so on the Monday following this first weekend of victory he showed up in front of his speech coach's desk, a trophy in each hand. The coach looked up at the beaming and proud kid and said, "You're not that good." Ouch. But time would prove that the coach was right. Raw talent is simply that, raw, until it gets cultivated, honed, and refined through focused diligence, dedicated effort, and a lot of hard work.

> "Achieving wins early on may be an example of 'luck' in play, but maintaining win after win means that hard work is combined with talent and unending desire."

Achieving wins early on may be an example of "luck" in play, but maintaining win after win means that hard work is combined with talent and unending desire.

Throughout four years of high school this young man won speech tournament after speech tournament, almost on a weekly basis. His name regularly was announced in the school paper and stories of his winning appeared in local newspapers as well. The trophies that proved his accomplishments were displayed conspicuously by his parents in their home. They were rightfully proud of their son, and he was proud, too, but not really in a haughty way. He was a hero to many, but was also misunderstood to a significant degree.

During his 9th grade year a local service club sponsored an all-boys international speech tournament. The first place prize was a $2,000.00 scholarship. Over 40,000 boys, ages 15 and 16, entered the contest. This tournament was composed of multiple levels. Only winning at each level, achieving a first place victory every time, would allow a contestant to continue to compete at the next level.

Beginning at the local club level, the teenage speaker achieved his first victory as he presented his oration and won first place. The speech was an original composition, five minutes in length, memorized, and presented without the use of a podium.

At subsequent levels the same speech was presented to larger crowds and remarkably, finally, the young man made it to the semi-final round in Portland, Oregon. The semi-final round consisted of five groups of eight speakers each. A total of 40,000 contestants had been reduced through competition to a top tier of 40. From these five groups of eight speakers, five winners would compete in the final round.

Maybe it was fate, bad luck, lack of experience, or insufficient preparation, but the competitive teenager didn't make it to the final round. He was beaten.

Back stage a red phone had been set up as a direct line to his home club from Southern California. The intent was that the youthful contestant would use that red phone to tell the members of the club assembled on the other end of the line that he had won. Well, he hadn't won, so he used this opportunity to tell them the truth and to tell them what was coming.

You see, the rules of this speech tournament stated that only boys of ages 15 and 16 years old could compete. He was 15. He had another year. He told the club he was grateful for their encouragement and support and then he vowed to try again.

The second year of high school came and with it the opportunity to make good on his promise to reenter the contest, and this year happened to be the 50th Anniversary of the founding of the service club.

The framework of competition was the same. Win at every level to go on to the next. Astonishingly, after several weeks of competition, the young speaker found himself again in the semi-final round, this time in Louisville, Kentucky. He won the semi-final round and made it into the final round. This semi-final round victory was amazing. Though there was no red phone this time, the elation was strong and the celebration sweet.

But it was short lived, not because it wasn't deserved or enjoyed, but because there was still work to do! A final round competition loomed the next day.

Thousands of convention goers were crowded into an indoor sports arena for the final round. The five finalists took their positions on the stage. One contestant after the other spoke to the crowd. Each was applauded as he finished his speech and returned to his seat. The air was thick with pride, anticipation, and excitement.

While the judges convened and scores were totaled, the boys and their sponsors or coaches retired back stage. Standing in a semicircle they soon noticed that the judges made an appearance. They stopped to talk with each contestant for a minute or two and then moved on to the next. When they came to the one who was the only returnee, they looked at him and said, "Nice speech." Then silence. That was all. That was it! Nothing more than two words, and the young man answered, "Thank you." What was he to think? What would *you* think?

The winner was to be announced shortly thereafter and all five contestants gathered on stage again, this time in silence, this time awaiting a decision from the judges. The speaking was done—their efforts were concluded. It was up to other people now to decide the winners or losers in this contest.

The winners of fifth and fourth places were announced. Third place followed. After that, there were two left: our "returnee" and one other competitor. Heaven and earth seemed to connect and eternity was swallowed up in an instant as the announcement of second place was made. The 16-year old returnee stayed in his seat. He had won the entire contest out of a pool of 40,000 young men. The crowd was on its feet in a standing ovation and this teenage competitor relished a degree of exhilaration he had never known before. It was an unbelievable experience. He was ecstatic and awestruck. Walking to the podium, he received the trophy. Turning to the crowd, he thanked the judges, the club, and his competition, praising their achievements. But there was only one winner, and he knew it, and he knew it was him.

He received the $2,000.00 scholarship. His parents were overjoyed. His sponsoring club cheered back home as the news spread quickly.

Returning to San Diego's Lindbergh Field this winning orator was met at the bottom of the tarmac with local news media cameras and about a hundred kids his age from his local church youth group, including the pastor of the church. All were cheering and applauding as he came off of the plane. Nothing had quite prepared him for this welcome or these accolades. And nothing quite prepared him for what was to happen during subsequent days, either.

His friends, except for a very few, began to isolate him. He was shunned … in the wake of victory.

The isolation was so marked that he made some choices. He decided he would never lessen himself to become a victim of the jealousy of others. He also chose to become the person who would eventually lead his peers. And in two years he became the President of the largest church youth group in his city.

The story could conclude here except for one additional segment that has to be told. During his senior year of high school this same youth was given another opportunity with a second international service club to compete in their speech tournament, but this one was for boys and girls. This one also was structured on multiple levels where winning was required at every level to keep competing, and this tournament also awarded a $2,000.00 scholarship to the first place winner.

This young competitor entered and won at each level, and soon found himself at the semifinal round in Reno, Nevada. He competed there and remarkably made it into the final round. He competed there. And he won, again. Once more he received a scholarship and the accolades that came with this victory.

But this time he decided to avoid the notoriety and overt public displays of victory. Instead, he requested of his parents and local sponsoring club that media not be present upon his arrival home. Although local radio interviews occurred, he wanted to go about his business as a leader of his peers. He was secure within himself and felt he didn't want or need a spotlight on this second achievement.

Staying out of this spotlight may have been a wrong or a right decision. Regardless, this teenager saw opportunity, went for it, used his God-given abilities, worked unbelievably hard, and won two championships. Possibly he may be the only person ever to win two international speech tournaments from service club organizations as a high school student.

Win and what happens? It's always a balance. Joy and well deserved pride of accomplishment are likely going to be combined with jealousy and ostracism from people who can't stand it when others do well.

Negative attitudes and actions from a few other people did not affect the outcomes. Winners continue to achieve and dedicate themselves to becoming all they can become, and often lead others to become the best people and contributors they can be. Because leadership abhors a vacuum, winners win and lead, no matter what. The story concludes:

> Here's the truth: become all you are or are destined to become. You stand a much greater chance of building what will last for yourself and those around you. The efforts are worth it if you are convinced your hard work matters. Remain strong even though barbs of jealousy, criticism, and isolation may be thrown your way when you win.

> Winning, especially where it is defined as becoming the best you can be no matter the odds, is a noble goal regardless of what people of lesser character think, say, or do. Define the win for yourself. Don't allow jealousy from those who refuse to try at all, to frame your success with their failures. You are better than that.

Ambition does not or should not drive a leader of a great cause. A leader is driven first by his or her *desire*—what he or she wants, based on what he or she is convinced is right: lofty morals, right standing, and the worth and truth of a cause. And *then* <u>the leader creates personal ambition</u> and drives to achieve the goal of fulfillment. In other words, ambition is a *choice and, like personality, is driven by the desires of the individual.*

Determination is not optional, nor is giving up. Ambition for a just cause and the actions taken to achieve fulfillment become verified results. It's not just about winning an award, becoming Number One, or taking the top prize. It's more than competing where one goal might be to see competitors lose—the ultimate benefit should be that of helping others. Ambition and the energy it requires to finish well have their places, of course; but a person can be ambitious about destroying other's lives, too. A word of caution: be mindful how you use the voice you'll gain with the wins you accomplish.

Raw ambition without right moral standing, wisdom, and an ultimate desire to benefit others can create immense destruction of people's lives, professional standings, and reputations. Ambition on a higher plain emerges from heartfelt desires to assist, not inhibit or destroy. Ambition on this plane also willingly depends on God and His plans of love. Ambition on this level is about completing more than competing.

What kind of ambition did Lincoln possess to become the President of the United States? He was quoted in 1860, for the first time, that he was thinking about running for President. He made his inclination public in a letter to someone he may not have trusted, but knew the "word" would get out. It did. The journey was set.

The account of Lincoln answering a question about whether he wanted to run for the highest office of the country is recounted in many public domain sources. Lincoln wrote, "The taste is in my mouth a little." On the basis of his character and brilliance already displayed, how could Lincoln not know upon declaring this that he was revealing his earnest desire for a position of leadership and the challenges, opportunities, and responsibilities that would accompany it?

The byline of this book is *The Making of a Leader*. Clearly, Lincoln became a leader. Some, actually many would say a great leader. But we know his personal life was flawed, his marriage difficult, his history "checkered," his formal education virtually non-existent.

Processes of making a superb leader often will present roles, some familiar, and some completely new for which preparation may not have been made. Great leaders "in the making" may choose to assume leadership roles because they're planned, or they may be pushed into leadership responsibilities by circumstances.

It is not easy to lead. Nor, perhaps, should it be. The making of a leader at some point will *require* an individual's true assessment of his or her personal qualifications as well as preparation, talents, gifting, personality, and the "readiness" to lead. I believe that true and lasting leadership at its core is not determined by title, status, tenure, or position. Rather, first of all, it emerges from desire for meritorious reasons. Hard work and sacrifice follow.

> Please see *Leadership Is – How to Build Your Legacy* by the author. www.LeadershipIs.com

The making of a leader involves a process where "one size" definitely does not fit all. Leadership for people who choose to lead or have roles and opportunities thrust upon them that require them to "step up" will exhibit traits unique to them. It is not possible to categorize everyone; no two are alike. It is possible, however, to help a leader understand if he or she is leading well.

7
Overcoming—
Understanding Call and Capability

A personal examination of a leader, or of one who aspires to leadership, or must assume leadership roles, may be a beneficial exercise. This process can help ascertain whether a person may be called as well as capable of leading others.

How much do you believe leaders can be called to lead? Or, how possible is it for a leader to think he or she is called but fail miserably because leadership traits and results are not evident? Was Lincoln "called" to become a leader? How important are the combinations of raw talent, potential, capability, timing, and luck when what is most needed is the hard work of preparation?

Whether things are going well or not, degrees of call or capability become evident, both to the leader and those who follow. Circumstances, good or bad, become the demonstration moments when true colors of character are revealed.

Leaders will face challenges whenever they desire to win, and they know they could experience losses in trying. Every opportunity is accompanied by at least one challenge.

And every opportunity may not necessarily represent a good option to pursue. Leaders know or soon learn this.

When presented with "new" requirements to lead, great leaders determine a wise course of action based on solid facts and factors. Among them is correct positioning of a leader's potential from his or her Call or Capability lists. Perhaps this concept is new to you. See if and how much it may resonate.

Here's a bottom line: leaders are more successful and fruitful when their actions emerge from understandings of their call and capability. When this knowledge is combined with earnest desire, a foundation of wisdom (knowing what to do and how to do it) and achieving successful results (doing jobs well) is built.

Great leaders purposefully and wisely limit the number of opportunities in which they choose to engage, putting efforts into those that are worthwhile, meritorious, meaningful, and showing the most promise of success. A person grows in leadership when he or she knows *how* to choose the best options from the list of opportunities, when to choose them, and why. Wasting time is never a preferred choice, so leaders review options and select their actions carefully.

When Lincoln declared in writing he was thinking about running for President, immense considerations must have come into play. In fact, remember that when he departed from Springfield after being elected, he referenced President Washington, stating that his (Lincoln's) task was greater than Washington's. He could only say that based on viable comparisons of historical accounts that he knew well.

Not everyone affected by his election was necessarily on the same "Lincoln team." One member of his personal support system, his wife, was more interested in her ascension to prominence through her husband than facing the momentous issues Lincoln as President had to confront on the national stage. Her desires were for social place and stature. In these defining moments of ascension to power, true colors of character, competence, and consistency shone through from many people close to the president.

Analyses from objective as well as subjective points of view which can be evidenced from comparing Call and Capability lists may be beneficial to a leader and those close to him or her. The goal is to assist in truth-telling, to allow genuine motives and actions to be aligned, while making sure efforts are expended on the most worthwhile objectives.

Activities a leader chooses to accomplish may be given greater merit as to their worth when analyses from utilizing a Call list or Capability list are employed. Sometimes a beneficial and meritorious activity can originate from both lists. Wisdom can help a person choose an activity based on "What I am called to do" versus "What I am capable of doing." This exercise is not a cake walk. In fact, the process can be tough.

Consider call and capability in more detail, especially if you are a leader. You are invited to view yourself in the descriptions and then judge how you spend the bulk of your time and energy. Lincoln didn't have this list or tool, of course. But these or similar considerations, I am sure, were not foreign to his analytical mind in combination with his keen sense of reason and desire.

Some people don't accept the concept of a "call" or "calling." Most everyone accepts the reality of capability, however. Whether or not one agrees with the concept of comparing call and capability, most agree with the need for ongoing education, preparation, and the experiences that should accompany personal growth.

Call and Capability

Activities you believe you are *called* to accomplish may not be the same as those you are *capable* of doing. Generally, the list of what a person is capable of doing is far longer than the list of what he or she may be called to do.

Ask yourself as you start to analyze your leadership contributions, "Am I acting more out of my Call List or my Capability List?"

Compare the lists with both eyes open, with a receptive heart, and a desire to learn. Put away discouragement and defensiveness if present. It's time to look, analyze, seek to understand, tell the truth to yourself, perhaps change your behaviors if judged appropriate to do so, and hopefully grow.

The differences between Call and Capability activities can be remarkable. Below are several comparisons. These are examples to consider. These are not "end all" descriptions. Indeed, some of them may not "fit" you at all.

Perhaps you can create your own lists and benefit from that exercise. None of these comparisons are to be seen as scientific, and none are ironclad. These considerations are designed to encourage an inquiring leader to think, delve deeper, agree, disagree, and choose actions that will help achieve growth in the person as well as the functions the person undertakes. Perhaps this exercise will help you.

Hopefully the lists will encourage you to more deeply consider yourself: what kind of leader you want or choose to be, whether or not you possess a choice to alter behaviors to more accurately align with an enhanced, clearer understanding of your person, how you utilize your time, how best you fulfill your responsibilities, and how fulfilled you are in what you accomplish.

In short, great leaders will embrace deliberations like this (certainly not limiting their exposure to these lists alone) because they'll *want* to be the best contributors they can be, recognizing and responding to their talents, call, and capability, and will show a willingness if not an eagerness to change and grow, adapting "new views where they can be shown to be true views."

Is your leadership ready for a journey like this? Let's see. It may be best to share your opinions and reactions with other people you trust, those who will have your best interests at heart as you consider the descriptions and your responses to them. If you have a mentor or a network you trust, you may wish to avail yourself of these folks.

Call and Capability Comparisons

Call	Capability
Tasks I complete because I want to	Tasks I complete because I have to
Fulfillment	Busywork
Internal and External Satisfaction	Some Accomplishment, but Not a Win
Time flies	Time drags

Duties I Enjoy	Duties I Endure
Actions I Require of Myself	Actions Others Require of Me
I'm Inspired to Achieve	I'm Obligated to Produce
Commitments I Embrace	Commitments I Tolerate
Gratification	Frustration
Enthusiastic Involvement	Fear to Commit
A Sense of Lasting Value	A Sense of Temporal Value
Helping a Higher Cause	Spending Time on Insignificant Issues
Money Is Not the Primary Motive	Without Being Paid, I'd Quit
Desiring a Greater Mission	Self-Serving Drudgery
Eager to Help Others	Looking Out Only for Number One
Discovering Opportunities	Added Work without Potential for Growth

Energized	Drained
Completeness	Complacency
Meaningfulness	Mediocrity
Prepared, On Time, and Connected	Not Prepared, Late, and Disconnected
Thinking Through and Planning Well	Letting Whatever Happens, Happen
Achieving Victory through Hard Work	Justification: It's Okay if We Don't Make It
Motivated, Achieving New Goals	Mainly Content, Going through Routines
Trying Alternative Methods	Keeping the Status Quo
Enjoying the Challenge	Hiding in the Familiar

Achieving Balance

Consider these truths:
1. Rarely can one operate exclusively within a Call List. Attending responsibilities often require performing activities corresponding to both lists. Making efforts

to achieve balance between the two can be motivational and essential to wellbeing.
2. In a healthy balance, the higher the number of duties accomplished from a Call List, the more fulfilment one may realize.
3. Personal balance is chosen by each individual. Consider these percentages:
   a. Operating from 50% Call and 50% Capability, or from far greater Capability than Call: This state can be frustrating, energy-draining, and discouraging.
   b. Operating from 60% Call and 40% Capability: This balance can be rewarding.
   c. Operating from 70% Call and 30% Capability: This balance may be preferred as a goal.
4. How many of your activities fall within each list? What are your percentages?
5. If you would like to improve the balance of activities within your call or capability lists, what steps could you take to initiate that improvement?

If it is true that leadership is willing to venture forth, analyze, and change course where it can be proven that such change is warranted, how willing are you to confront your opportunities for growth and accompanying challenges, why are these efforts worth it, and when will you start?

Even though Lincoln may have never heard of call and capability in a format like this, he was clearly called to lead, he did lead, and the country was better for it, in spite of what it cost. Distractions were not allowed to rule. Personality traits were not to drive him or dissuade him from the larger goal. Overcoming is what he did, though the struggle from within may have been immense, and the struggle from without never ceased as long as he was president.

The desires to overcome and the backbone to choose actions to make right goals happen are characteristics of a great leader. How much do you want to grow in your leadership, beginning with recognizing what actions you believe you are called to accomplish versus those that are part of something you can do but may not be called to do? How willing might you be to realign your efforts if this realignment can be shown to be the right thing to do? What are your earnest desires in this regard?

You can readily see how important your choices are or will become when you are leading, no matter the size of your organization or what personality traits you possess. Especially when confronting immense, surmounting difficulties close to you or more removed, the confidence you possess from within, in combination with a healthy assessment of your character, and dependence upon God, will or should help you to know whether you are right for the role, and whether the role of leadership is right for you, and whether you are putting your efforts toward the right actions.

On pages 39 and 40 the concept of Core Team is presented. At this point, the "E" of Team is worth unpacking.

As noted, the "E" stands for Essentials of Your Composite Nature: what makes you, you. These are composed of your experience, education, and environment.

Think about Lincoln's composite nature, part of his person. How would you evaluate his experience in helping to prepare him for service in the highest office in the land, leading the country through the Civil War? Referenced before, he had to know what he was facing, at least in part, when he compared his role of serving as president to that of Washington.

Plus, his experience included a roller coaster of pluses and minuses ... we have named several. How would you evaluate your experiences as part of your preparation to lead, if leading is your task? No person's experiences are identical to another's; therefore your experiences, like Lincoln's, have helped to shape you, and will continue to.

By his own admission, Lincoln's education was severely lacking when young, but through personal development and in his professional years, including those in New Salem and Springfield, on the circuit, and in government, he studied — and studied often — he borrowed and read every book he could borrow. He *worked* at learning. He read constantly. His mind was sharp. It became sharper through multiple years and labors of mental stretching that his reading revealed, permitted, and encouraged. How diligently do you pursue avenues of learning, continuously?

There are at least two kinds of environments: ones created for you, and ones you create. Often they exist in combination. Leaders are tasked with understanding their environments, and perhaps molding them if need be. To degrees possible and advantageous for the right reasons, leaders may be destined to change an environment for the good.

In what kinds of environments are you most contributory? What kinds of environments challenge you? Which environments must you overcome, challenge, and even change?

The exercise of running for office includes a desire to change environments and provide new leadership. Basing these desires on moral truths of which a leader is convinced—much like Lincoln's inherent opposition to slavery—can reap immense good if the belief "in the right" is strong enough, fortitude is resilient enough, and persistence long enough to see a worthwhile goal through to completion.

We can conclude that Lincoln's character was strong, his beliefs unwavering, and that regardless of a history of personal difficulty or personality traits deemed difficult, he rose to the challenge and overcame the obstacles in his path. Such is a demonstration of leadership, indeed perhaps "called" leadership. It's never without some degree of sacrifice, remember that.

If the cause is great enough for any leader, if it's meritorious enough for you if you are the leader, you can desire to overcome obstacles for the greater good. How strong is that desire and how hard do you want to work? Are you called to lead? How much do you achieve balance between call and capability in the analysis of how you spend your time?

Time will tell you and others around you whether you are the right leader for the right job in the right place at the right time with sufficient strength of character within your person to see it through. Perhaps you will soar like an eagle in your leadership.

8
Closing Thoughts

When I was about eleven years old I became fascinated with the story of the life of Abraham Lincoln. That fascination and the desire to learn the principles and practices of leadership from his life's example grew exponentially and have not abated.

The more I've learned, the more I want to learn. Perhaps you are one of these people with an insatiable desire for knowledge. Knowing truths is the beginning, of course; but applying them — creating action steps because of your desire to change your behavior for the better — must follow if learning is to become living.

Hopefully you and I have shared truths in this book which you may find helpful. What changes do you desire to make so that what you've learned becomes new action within your life? I wish you well on your journey.

Lincoln Sculpture, Lincoln Plaza, Springfield, Illinois, April, 2017

The Lincoln Home, Springfield, Illinois, April, 2017

About the Author

Glen Aubrey

Author, Publisher, Professional Musician, Emmy ® Award Winner, Consultant

www.glenaubrey.com

Creative Team Publishing (CTP): CTP publishes many of the country's most successful and influential authors, **www.CreativeTeamPublishing.com.** Through CTP, Glen has released twelve books of his own dealing with leadership and team development; the life, leadership, and legacy of Abraham Lincoln; Gettysburg Civil War history; and two poetry books. Formed in 2007, CTP publishes fiction and nonfiction books on diverse topics. Among them:

- Medical malpractice and the law
- Resilience through difficult times
- Health care fundamentals, transformation, and leadership
- Military service and veterans
- Law enforcement, policing standards, and undercover operations
- Inner city
- Children's novels
- Parenting
- Drug abuse and addiction

About the Author

- Political issues
- Investment in people for life change
- Children with special needs
- Inspirational, motivational, and encouraging stories
- Faith, belief, and practice
- Experiencing and dealing with grief
- Poetry
- Team building
- Business organizational structure and operations
- United States History, Civil War, and Lincoln

Creative Music Enterprises (CME): CME was formed in 1976, **www.CreativeMusicEnterprises.com.** The company provides custom compositions and orchestrations; performances; album writing, arranging and production; commercials (music and voiceovers); music publishing; and advertising. Through this firm, Glen won an Emmy ® in 2012 as the composer for a television commercial.

Creative Team Resources Group (CTRG) Building Relationships—Making More: a consulting and leadership training firm, **www.ctrg.com.** CTRG specializes in building Core Teams, internal structures that produce strength and productivity within the person and the firm. Among CTRG's clientele:
1. Directorate of Admissions, United States Military Academy, West Point, New York
2. U.S. Department of Veterans Affairs, Washington, D.C.

About the Author

3. State of California Department of Transportation (Caltrans), District 6, Fresno, California
4. TomaTek (food processing and manufacturing), Firebaugh, California
5. S. C. Johnson, Fresno, California
6. County of San Diego, California, Health and Human Services Agency (HHSA): Director's Office, Fiscal, Accounting, Information Technology, Facilities Management, Alcohol and Drugs
7. Whirlpool Corporation, Benton Harbor, Michigan
8. Fujitsu America: Computer and IT Sales and Service
9. Northrup Grumman, San Diego, California
10. Fresno Water District, Fresno, California
11. American Society of Consultant Pharmacists, Alexandria, Virginia
12. Salem Communications, San Diego, California

Creative Ministry Teams (CMT): CMT is a 501 (c) (3) non-profit organization, **www.CreativeMinistryTeams.org.** CMT serves universities, schools, theater groups, churches, and other non-profits, to develop leadership and build Core Teams. Among CMT's clients:
1. Grand Canyon University, Phoenix, Arizona
2. YFC/Campus Life, San Diego, California
3. Forest Home Conference Center, Forest Falls, California
4. Thousand Pines Conference Center, Crestline, California
5. Town Hall Arts Center, Littleton, Colorado

6. Churches and non-profit organizations in Southern California and Phoenix, Arizona
7. Programming Arts Team (PAT) development for hundreds of Core Teams and their members in churches, schools, and theater groups across the United States. A PAT consists of leadership and teams within these fields:
    a. Music
    b. Media
    c. Drama
    d. Technical Services
    e. Support Services
    f. Administration
    g. Stage Design/Artistic Direction

Personal: "I enjoy traveling, especially to Gettysburg, Washington, D.C., Europe, and the Middle East. I treasure multi-cultural experiences and am fulfilled when conducting conference center presentations and speaking engagements. Enjoyments in life include walking, bicycle riding, and being with family and close friends; also a fireplace, my dogs, listening to classical music and profound artistic works. I appreciate, compose, and arrange multiple styles of music. I earnestly engage in creatively stimulating conversations on uplifting topics, listening and responding to other people's well thought-out perspectives. I love to laugh. I thoroughly enjoy good football and baseball games. I am a student and teacher, a follower and leader."

Products and Services

You are invited to contact Glen Aubrey and his teams for products and services.

www.glenaubrey.com

<u>Book Publishing</u>
Creative Team Publishing (CTP)
If you are an author: "We Want to Publish Your Book!"
www.CreaativeTeamPublishing.com

<u>Music Performance, Production, Promotion, Publishing</u>
Creative Music Enterprises (CME)
www.creativemusicenterprises.com

<u>Conferences, Consultation, and Coaching</u>
Creative Team Resources Group (CTRG)
Building Relationships. Making More.
www.ctrg.com

<u>Non-Profit Organization</u>
<u>Conferences, Consultation, and Coaching</u>
Creative Ministry Teams (CMT)
www.creativeministryteams.org

*****

Acknowledgments

Family and friendships are treasures. Watching young family members grow and investing in extended family are unbelievable delights. And throughout the years, many people have become and remain very close friends. I truly enjoy my family and friends.

Time is precious. How it is spent, of course, is a choice each person makes consistently. Some people who aspire to be authors occasionally say to me, "I don't know if I have the time to write my book..." to which I often reply, "We all have the same amount of time every day." I smile when I say it. Then I encourage them to write their thoughts out, whether or not publishing is their ultimate goal.

Others who have heard my music, live or recorded, have on occasion commented, "I wish I could play like that..." a sincere compliment I humbly accept. Then I ask them, again smiling, "How hard do you want to work?"

Accomplishment takes devotion, dedicated time, hard work, commitment, and most of all, desire. Yes, talent helps. Talents are blessings we often don't deserve. Those who have been blessed with gifts of God should be grateful. Gratitude is a choice. Being grateful remains part and parcel of my thought processes and activities on very nearly a daily basis. *Then* I get to the *work* of practicing and perfecting what God has entrusted to me. There will be days when the work seems too hard, too long, overly arduous, and at times unfulfilling. *Then* I renew my resolve and push harder. This is not arrogance; it is a desire to become the best I can become, fulfilling what I believe is a call from God.

So let me acknowledge the Source of all gifting: God. I am truly grateful to Him. Then let me acknowledge the "will to work" taught to me by my parents, which hopefully I am passing on to my children and their children. I love seeing my children and their families walk and serve in truth, love, and obedience to God. I encourage them in this; I always will.

Encouraging others of family and friends has been a desire and activity of mine for a long time. Seeing other people succeed is a true joy, and helping them if they want my help, is an honor.

I acknowledge that I am unable and actually unwilling to "go it alone" if achieving "solo" equates to an unbalanced and arrogant display of self-fulfillment. Life for me constitutes a balance of at least these characteristics: choosing a grateful, joyful, and careful blending of gifting, hard work, positive attitudes, and strong relationships. In combination, these characteristics can produce the fulfillment of a cause and a grateful and gratified person as well.

In 2017, I offered to compose and record a simple yet heartfelt song for a friend. It is called "Joy Comes." Joy is a choice, a part of the process of growth, and becomes a result. While I love to have fun, and have fun enjoying exciting times in varied ways, I also realize that joy is a process as well as a product of fulfillment. It may include fun and happiness, or it may not. Joy is something deeper.

Here's a description of this song:

> **Joy Comes (2017)**
> Written and performed for a friend, this song was designed to show that through heart's desires, faith and belief, strong endeavors (hard work), and results (good or bad), joy comes. Joy in this sense represents fulfillment, not necessarily happiness, although it certainly doesn't exclude happiness. Joy is often a choice and made more so when times and circumstances are difficult. I choose joy. You can, too. One of our CTP authors expressed words like this often; she was (and is) right.

I acknowledge that I have a long way to go in learning what life is all about. I acknowledge that I am willing to work hard to achieve what I believe I am called to do. I also willingly and joyfully acknowledge dependence on God.

www.ingramcontent.com/pod-product-compliance
Lightning Source LLC
Chambersburg PA
CBHW022228010526
44113CB00033B/685